Appledore

THE RAILWAYS OF
SOUTH EAST ENGLAND

ANDREW KNIGHT

LONDON

IAN ALLAN LTD

Contents

First published 1986

ISBN 0 7110 1556 2

Published by Ian Allan Ltd, Shepperton, Surrey; and printed by Ian Allan Printing Ltd at their works at Coombelands in Runnymede, England

All uncredited photographs courtesy of Lens of Sutton.

Cover photograph by Hugh Ballantyne

Front endpaper
3B164   Appledore on 5 September 1984 as 'Hastings' DEMU No 1111 rolls in with an Ashford-Hastings working.

Rear endpaper
4B222   Betchworth, although the station remains open it has been unstaffed since November 1967.

How to use this Book

Railway enthusiasts and historians are fascinated by dates, and even the casual traveller can find his curiosity aroused by the sight of an overgrown station or a disused branch line glimpsed from a passing train.

The aim of this book is to provide answers to questions: what was a station called? When did it close? What community did it serve? Using maps, photographs and easy-to-read tables, the book provides a concise and logical source of reference that answers all such queries and builds up chapter by chapter to offer a definitive history of rail travel in the southeast of England.

The index provides an instant guide to the exact location of information about a specific line or station, and the passenger, rambler or researcher can then refer quickly to a potted history of the railway in question.

The area covered by the 'South Eastern' network is divided into seven 'regions', each with their own maps. The geographical regions are then sub-divided into lines, with brief introductory notes providing information about ownership, opening and closure dates, and details of which sections of track remain open to freight or passenger traffic.

A concise table then gives opening and closure dates for each station on the line, followed by notes about changes of name, freight traffic and other important facilities.

For anybody travelling by train in southeast England or exploring the old, forgotten lines, the book is an invaluable companion, bringing history alive.

It is instantly possible to ascertain whether a small halt was opened by the Southern Railway in the 1930s, or was part of an SER expansion plan: whether a station closed during the Beeching era or had lost its services 50 years earlier.

For the first time, detailed tables giving the opening and closing dates of an entire railway system have been brought together, providing the reader with a ready supply of instant answers to familiar questions.

And with the book readily at hand, history jumps out of each deserted platform and disused trackbed. It is a complex and intriguing story, and one in which every date has its own tale to tell.

The dates in this book have been checked against dozens of sources, old and new. Inevitably, with thousands of snippets of information included, there are missing details and in some cases dates are contested, or forgotten. The author would welcome any correspondence designed to update the information provided or correct any inaccuracies that arise.

Andrew Knight
Aberdeen

3B172   SR Class 202 Hastings units running ECS through St Leonards (Warrior Square) on 28 August 1977. *Les Bertram*

Dates

This book contains thousands of carefully researched dates, which in most cases refer to officially recognised opening and closure details. Textual notes identify where dates have been obtained from timetables or other sources, and separate dates are given in cases where lines and stations opened to the public at different times from the official, or ceremonial opening.

Where normal services stopped prior to official closure, or continued beyond it, alternative dates are given below tables. In many cases, line and station closures officially dated from a Monday, while the actual last trains operated on the preceding Saturday: in these examples, the Monday date of closure is included.

Over the years, a number of dates have been contested by authors who have obtained their information from different sources – and in some cases inaccuracies have been compounded by later writers accepting information without checking it against contemporary sources.

Every effort has been made to ensure that the details published in the following chapters are correct.

Tables

Key to tables

Column 1: Number of station (for indexing and reference purposes).

Column 2: Name of station (original name as at opening date; subsequent names are included in the notes underneath each table). An asterisk in this column indicates that notes about the station are included in the information printed beneath the table. The letter ® confirms that the station was renamed, details of subsequent names being printed below the table.

Column 3: The public opening date of the station.

Column 4: Date of closure to passengers, if appropriate. Stations which remain open to passengers are listed giving their full present name.

Column 5: Date of closure to goods, if appropriate. A horizontal line indicates that a station did not support goods services. A dagger symbol indicates that a station remains open to goods – if the dagger follows a closure date, this indicates that some facilities remain open – eg private sidings.

Column 6: Final closure date, if appropriate. A letter P indicates a station which remains open to passengers, and G for goods.

Abbreviations

Station details

P	passengers (used with opening & closure dates)
G	goods (used with opening & closure dates)
CC	completely closed
®	renamed
O	opened
RO	reopened
c	ceremonial opening date
p	public opening date
g	opened to goods
N/A	date not available
TC	temporarily closed
PC	permanently closed
t	date as indicated from timetables
CDO	coal depot only
CCD	coal concentration depot
EMU	electric multiple-unit

Company details

BREL	British Rail Engineering Ltd
CP&SLJR	Crystal Palace & South London Junction Railway
C&W	Canterbury & Whitstable Railway
EKR	East Kent Railway
ELJR	East London Joint Railway
G&R	Gravesend & Rochester Railway
GER	Great Eastern Railway
GWR	Great Western Railway
L&BR	London & Brighton Railway
L&CR	London & Croydon Railway
L&GR	London & Greenwich Railway
LBSCR	London, Brighton & South Coast Railway
LCDR	London, Chatham & Dover Railway
LNWR	London & North Western Railway
LSWR	London & South Western Railway
LT	London Transport
MetRy	Metropolitan Railway
RHDR	Romney, Hythe & Dymchurch Railway
SR	Southern Railway
SER	South Eastern Railway
SECR	South Eastern & Chatham Railway
VS&PR	Victoria Station & Pimlico Railway
WELCPR	West End of London & Crystal Palace Railway
WLER	West London Extension Railway

How the Network Developed

Early Days

The pickings looked rich for the early railway promoters when they first contemplated ventures in the southeast of England. They saw an area of immense potential, bounded on one side by the busy metropolis of London and on the other by the flourishing ports of the Kent coast, with a number of tempting towns lying in between. Coupled with the public's growing desire for increased mobility, this was a combination of attractions appearing to hold the key to a successful and rapidly-expanding railway system, but the early speculators were not to know, of course, that the big companies which were to later criss-cross the county of Kent with railway lines would find the Garden of England a commercial battlefield and a bed of thorns.

The foundations of the South Eastern Railway's network were laid with the opening of two independent lines, the Canterbury & Whitstable Railway (1A) in 1830 and the London & Greenwich Railway (5C) into London Bridge in 1836, the same year that the South Eastern's own Act was passed. The inhabitants of Canterbury had long wanted better access to the sea than the existing roads allowed, and the proposal for a railway to Whitstable was put forward in 1823 by William James, a once rich and powerful man who had already projected a number of railways and who had been the first promoter of the Liverpool & Manchester Railway. However, financial embarrassment and failing health forced him to drop out of the railway business, and it was George Stephenson who became the engineer in charge of building the six-mile long, single-track line.

Three types of power were sanctioned for use on the railway: stationary engines, horses and steam locomotives, and all were used to convey passengers over different sections of the route. Stationary engines hauled trains up the line's three steep gradients, with coaches and wagons allowed to descend inclines at low speed under their own weight. The pioneer locomotive *Invicta*, built by Robert Stephenson & Co and brought by sea from Newcastle, took trains along the last two miles into Whitstable – and the engine's entry into service in the spring of 1830 meant that the Canterbury & Whitstable beat both the Liverpool & Manchester and Stockton & Darlington railways to become the first railway to carry passengers on locomotive-hauled trains. *Invicta* was only around the 70th railway engine to be built, and was the first to feature outside cyclinders at the leading end, which later became a popular arrangement.

The line itself cost around £110,000 to build, with trains passing half-way along the route, at Clowes Wood. Horses were used on the level stretch when *Invicta* was put out of commission, but locomotive working was adopted throughout in April 1846. Whitstable Harbour opened in 1832, and from 1836 a steamer was operated from London every other day, with trains being timed to connect with it.

After unsuccessful attempts to lease the line, an agreement was finally reached with the South Eastern Railway in 1844, and from that time the SER worked the route – buying it outright in 1853.

The London & Greenwich Railway had the distinction of being the first railway in London, receiving Royal Assent in 1833 and opening to the public between Deptford and London Bridge in 1836. That original stretch of line was a mere 3¾ miles long and practically level, having been constructed throughout on a viaduct of 878 arches. A temporary station at Greenwich was reached in 1838 and from 1839, London & Croydon trains began running over the line between Corbett's Lane and London Bridge, following the opening of the Croydon company's 8¾-mile line to what is now West Croydon.

At London Bridge, a new station was constructed for L&C trains just north of the Greenwich terminus, but the companies exchanged their stations in 1844 because of operating difficulties. In 1841, the London & Brighton Railway opened its line to Norwood, and its trains ran over Croydon and Greenwich metals into London Bridge.

The London & Greenwich had cost around £260,000 a mile to build, and originally trains were worked by the company's own fleet of nine locomotives. But the SER leased and worked the line from 1845, although the L&G company was not finally dissolved until the Grouping in 1923.

The Birth of the South Eastern Railway

The South Eastern Railway, meantime, had been sanctioned to build a line that connected with the London & Brighton at Reigate (now Redhill) and ran east through Tonbridge, Maidstone and Ashford to Folkestone and Dover. It was not the company's first choice of route, but the Government had suggested that rather than opening a line from London to Folkestone and Dover via Oxted, as originally proposed, the SER and the L&B should share tracks as far as Earlswood Common. The outcome was that the Brighton company built its line and the South Eastern bought a small section, exercising running powers over the northern portion into London. The Oxted route would have been more direct, but would have required heavy engineering. However, operating two main-line services over the same line for such a long distance was bound to lead to a souring of relationships between the two companies involved – and the mutual antipathy later grew more acute when the South Eastern took to starting trains out of London only a few minutes before its rival's fast services were due to leave.

It was 1842 when the first South Eastern trains started running into London from Tonbridge (4A), traversing Brighton and Croydon metals from Reigate. The purchase of the Brighton line between Coulsdon and Reigate (4C) was finally agreed in 1845 after a lengthy dispute. A few months after Tonbridge had opened, the main line was successfully extended to Ashford (3A), running practically straight and almost dead level. Folkestone was reached in 1843, but a temporary station had to be used while the Foord

Viaduct was built – reaching a maximum height of 1,000ft and crossing the valley through which a mill stream ran on its way to the harbour.

Between Folkestone and Dover (1G), engineer William Cubitt faced a new challenge in the shape of the lofty chalk cliffs. The construction of a series of tunnels and cuttings involved a considerable amount of difficult and expensive engineering work, and at one point, between the Abbot's Cliff and Shakespeare tunnels, Cubitt had to blow up the towering obstacle of the Round Down cliff.

Folkestone Harbour had been built by Telford in 1809, but was never a success, and the South Eastern was able to buy it for £18,000 in 1843, linking it to the main line with a goods branch in the same year. The Harbour station was over 100ft below the junction, and the line boasted an average gradient of 1 in 36, which on some occasions led to four engines being used to propel trains, two pushing and two pulling. Heavier engines could not be used on the branch because of the limited capacity of the swing bridge over the entrance to the inner harbour.

The line was opened to passengers after five years of use as a goods line on 1 Janaury 1849. Meanwhile, the main line had reached its new terminus at Dover Town (1G) in 1844, an event which transformed the overland carriage of foreign mail. It was a period of radical change for the port, for although steamships had replaced sailing boats earlier in the century, nearly all overland traffic to and from London had taken the line of the 'Dover Road', a journey dramatically described by Charles Dickens in *A Tale of Two Cities*. The arrival of the railway revolutionised the journey to London, and also heralded major expansion and improvement work at Dover Harbour itself.

Back in London, the new Greenwich station – formerly the Croydon company's terminus – was to form the basis of the South Eastern's own London Bridge station, which was enlarged in 1850 and finally completed in 1851. The new terminus at Bricklayers Arms (5G), opened jointly by the South Eastern and London & Croydon companies, was dubbed the 'Grand West-End Terminus of the South Eastern Railway' but never lived up to its name. It was closed to passengers in 1852, and all interest in the line as a possible passenger route into London died with the opening of Charing Cross in 1864.

Meanwhile the London & Brighton and London & Croydon companies teamed up with three other railways in 1846 to form the London, Brighton & South Coast Railway, whose developing network of lines was to mark, for the most part, the western boundary of the South Eastern's territory.

Out in the Kent countryside, the South Eastern opened its 10-mile long branch from Maidstone Road (Paddock Wood) to Maidstone (2K) in 1844. The single track followed the course of the River Medway and was equipped with electric telegraph – the use of which was extended all over the South Eastern system two years later. The branch was soon doubled, and despite offering only a circuitous route to London, soon put paid to the road competition offered by the coaches.

The short branch line from Tonbridge to Tunbridge Wells (3C) was opened in 1845, running uphill all the way, and was quickly followed by the main line from Ashford to Canterbury, Ramsgate and Margate (1B) in

1846, the branch to Deal (1E) being completed in 1847.

Way back in 1824 a canal had been built linking the Thames and Medway between Gravesend and Rochester, and consisting of two long tunnels separated by a short open stretch. A single track had been laid along the canal towpath in 1845 by the Gravesend & Rochester Railway (2A), but in 1846 the SER bought the line and the following year filled in the canal to build a double-track railway between Denton and Strood as part of its North Kent line. The line opened throughout in 1849, when Denton was linked to North Kent Junction (5E), slightly west of Greenwich on the old L&G line. The birth of the North Kent Railway was to prove of great strategic importance to the South Eastern, and moved its centre of gravity considerably further north.

Although most South Eastern interests were tightly contained, another line opened in 1849 which was to bring the company's engines clean through Brighton and London & South Western territory into the Great Western's sphere of operations at Reading. The independent Reading, Guildford & Reigate Railway opened throughout in 1849 and was worked by the South Eastern from its inception. The larger company bought it over completely in 1852 (4B). The bad gradients and tortuous route meant that few passengers from London would be tempted to use it in preference to the broad gauge, but because it offered a direct route to Aldershot Camp, it acquired considerable military value.

To the south, the South Eastern and Brighton companies began squabbling over territory again outside Hastings. The LBSCR line from Lewes to St Leonards had opened in 1846, and the SER had permission to extend this to Hastings, which it duly did in 1851, the same year that the line from Ashford to Hastings was completed (3B). The Brighton company was irate that the South Eastern's tunnel at Bopeep was so narrow that it had to be worked as single line, even though it carried two tracks, and the following year the South Eastern opened another route to Hastings, this time from Tunbridge Wells, via Robertsbridge and Battle, adding further heat to the dispute. Relations between the two companies were further strained in 1856 by the opening of the independent Caterham railway (4E): neither the Brighton nor the Croydon companies wished the bother of working it, but they were equally unwilling to see its traffic being won by a competitor. When it opened the line was worked by the LBSCR, but it was bought by the South Eastern in 1859, when a new problem arose over whether passengers from the branch should travel on to London from Godstone Road (later Purley) in Brighton or South Eastern trains. The vicious battle for custom was not contained to the company boardroom, either, but spilled onto the platforms where station staff became involved in some undignified struggles in their efforts to win over passengers. At the time of opening, the branch was a pleasant rural route with only modest passenger potential. In later years, the development of the surrounding area into pleasant, wooded suburbia ensured the line a secure future.

With the years of violent expansion at an end, the South Eastern's next task was to tie up some loose ends – including the extension of its North Kent line from Strood to Maidstone in 1856 (2L). Ironically, it was also to be Strood which became the focus of attention for the East Kent Railway, which had been incorporated in 1853 and now had ambitious plans for a new railway to Canterbury.

The Arrival of the London, Chatham & Dover Railway

The promoters of the East Kent Railway had good reasons for thinking that their investment in a line from Rochester to Canterbury would bring them prosperity. With the line completed, they could then promote a shorter route to Dover, similar to one that had been foreseen 15 years earlier before the South Eastern route was completed. The East Kent Railway opened from Strood to Faversham in 1858 (2D), and although the ambitious undertaking proved an uphill struggle, it was extended to Dover by 1861 (1J). The company's Act allowed it to use the South Eastern stations at Strood and Canterbury, and when the East Kent agreed that the line would start at Strood, the South Eastern gave a valuable undertaking that it would not in any future session oppose any bill introduced for powers to construct the line onto Dover. At the time, the South Eastern directors saw the East Kent strictly as an extension of their North Kent line rather than as a major rival. Had they known at that stage that the East Kent would subsequently seek an independent line to London, they would doubtless have been more circumspect – and taken action that would have changed irrevocably the pattern of railway development in Kent. As it was, the South Eastern was confident that it held the strategic advantage by being able to channel all land traffic from Europe over its own metals.

The shock came in 1856, when the East Kent opened its attack on London with a proposal for a new line via Lewisham to link up with the West End of London & Crystal Palace Railway. Thoroughly rattled, the South Eastern opposed the granting of running powers over its line from Strood to Dartford, where the proposed new railway would diverge. It's opposition was successful – but not for long, since in 1858 the East Kent obtained powers to extend west from Strood to Bickley (2D) to join the Mid-Kent Railway's line from Bromley to Bickley (6F), which was opened that year along with the Farnborough Extension of the West End

of London & Crystal Palace Railway (6E) from Norwood to Bromley.

These developments gave the East Kent access to Battersea along the line already built by the WEL&CPR – and there the Victoria Station & Pimlico Railway was building a line across the Thames to a new terminus at Victoria (7A), which also opened in 1858. When the line from Rochester Bridge to Bickley was eventually opened in 1860, the East Kent – re-named the London, Chatham & Dover Railway in 1859 – suddenly had direct access to London over a series of different companies' lines.

The Farnborough extension was leased to the Chatham in 1859 and absorbed into it in 1862; the Mid-Kent was leased to the company from 1862; and from 1861 it received a joint lease with the Great Western of half of Victoria station from the VS&PR. In 1860 the Chatham got powers for a bold and expensive project that would give it independent access to Victoria, and the line from Herne Hill to Stewarts Lane Junction was opened in 1862, and extended to Beckenham the following year.

The South Eastern was not amused, even though stiff gradients and the uneven character of the Chatham's line from London to Dover severely handicapped it in competing for traffic. But worse was to follow, for the same Act that authorised the Chatham to extend its line to Victoria also permitted a new line to be built from Herne Hill into the heart of London at Blackfriars, and thence on to join the Metropolitan Railway at Farringdon Street (5A). The bold and expensive project was to open a series of connections with other railway companies that would pave the way for a sea of transfer traffic across London. The line opened to Elephant & Castle in 1862, reached a temporary station at Ludgate Hill in 1864 and was eventually joined to the Metropolitan Railway at West Street Junction in 1866.

2B82   Wybourne Sidings signalbox and 'C' class 0-6-0 No 31495 standing with a freight alongside High Halstow Halt on 9 July 1955.   *J. H. Aston*

In the early days, both the Great Northern and Metropolitan companies thought sufficiently highly of the Chatham's Blackfriars station that they wished to start many of their trains from there – and in return, the Chatham was offered the free use of Farringdon Street and Kings Cross stations. But Blackfriars closed to passengers in 1885, although the goods station continued in use for almost exactly 100 years.

If the ambitious expansion in South London was to cost the Chatham dear, it was also to seriously weaken the South Eastern, which was prompted to invest in a new line to Charing Cross in a bid to outdo its arch-rival. The railway had been promoted by an independent company and sanctioned in 1859, but amalgamation with the South Eastern took place in 1864.

Charing Cross opened that year, followed by another new terminus at Cannon Street in 1866 (5B), but the South Eastern paid a high price for the two new termini and their approach lines – some £4 million that it could ill-afford.

Meanwhile a number of new spurs and connecting lines had been added to the Chatham's network in South London in 1865-66, and the following year saw the opening of a new high level approach to Victoria (7A).

As if not satisfied with its new access routes to London, the South Eastern was splashing out even more money on the construction of a new main line from New Cross to Tonbridge which would offer much faster schedules between the Channel ports and the Charing Cross and Cannon Street termini. This new line was completed to Chislehurst in 1865 and and Tonbridge in 1868 (6A) and was characterised by long stretches of high embankment and several impressive brick bridges.

Another suburban money-spinner opened in 1866, the Dartford Loop Line from Hither Green (5H), while between 1873 and 1878 the South Eastern was also able to fill in the gap between Charlton and Greenwich on the Woolwich line (5D).

In 1865 a new branch line opened from Nunhead to Crystal Palace, worked by the Chatham company and terminating at the distinctive High Level station at Crystal Palace (6L).

At Sevenoaks, a nominally independent company had opened a line from Sevenoaks Junction (Swanley) to Sevenoaks (Bat & Ball) in 1862 (2H), which was also worked by the Chatham company, and which was extended to Tubs Hill in 1869 and from Otford to Maidstone in 1874.

The Bromley Direct Railway gave the South Eastern a new suburban branch to Bromley (North) in 1878 (6C), and the West Wickham & Hayes Railway was acquired in 1881, the line opening from Elmers End to Hayes in 1882 (6M).

Expansion and Consolidation

More lines followed at a steady pace as both companies continued to develop their networks in Kent. The Chatham's branch from Nunhead to Greenwich opened as far as Blackheath Hill in 1871 and was extended to Greenwich Park in 1888 (6J). The South Eastern's Sandgate branch – known as the Hythe & Sandgate Railway – opened in 1874 (1H), and in a rare spirit of co-operation the two companies joined forces to complete a joint line from Buckland Junction at Dover to Deal in 1881 (1F). The same year the South Eastern acquired and opened a picturesque railway between Dunton Green and Westerham, the Westerham Valley line, which to many people epitomised the character and atmosphere of the English branch (6B).

The Lydd Railway was another nominally independent concern, and was not vested in the South Eastern until 1895. But in 1881 the lonely line was opened across the desolate Romney Marshes from Appledore to Lydd and Dungeness (goods only). Passenger services to Dungeness were introduced in 1883 and the line opened to New Romney in 1884. Dungeness was intended to became a great port, but the dream never materialised and the bare landscape

5B266 A general view of Charing Cross station on 14 September 1977. *Brian Morrison*

was left in the charge of its population of resilient sheep.

An unhappy branch to Port Victoria opened in 1882, the delightfully-named Hundred of Hoo Railway having been acquired by the South Eastern the previous year. Once again, the port was a dismal failure in maritime terms, but its thriving industrial traffic in explosives, cement, chemicals and oil secured its future even after passenger services were finally withdrawn in 1961 (2B).

The Croydon, Oxted & East Grinstead Railway was a joint venture of the South Eastern and LBSCR, and linked South Croydon with Oxted in 1884, whence the Brighton company ran on alone to East Grinstead. The opening of a link between Hurst Green Junction and Ashurst Junction on the East Grinstead to Tunbridge Wells route gave the LBSCR a double-line route to Tunbridge Wells which competed closely with the South Eastern route. However, because the joint line also connected with the South Eastern's old main line, the SER was able to introduce a Tonbridge service over the Oxted route from 1886 (4G).

Meanwhile, despite strident South Eastern opposition, the Chatham was able to link Maidstone and Ashford in 1884 (2J), running to its own terminus at Ashford, but with powers to continue trains into the South Eastern station. Another invasion into South Eastern territory came with the opening of the Gravesend branch in 1886 (2E), but although this served the famous gardens at Rosherville, the line never thrived.

In response to its growing demands for more terminal space in London, the Chatham opened a new station at St Pauls in 1886 (5A), approached by a new bridge across the Thames.

A separate company had promoted a link between Woodside on the SER's Addiscombe Road branch and Selsdon Road which was sanctioned in 1880 and jointly acquired by the South Eastern and LBSCR in 1882. It was opened in 1885 and worked by the South Eastern.

The Elham Valley Railway (1K) was one of the unfortunate and ill-fated products of the intense competition that existed between the South Eastern and Chatham companies at this time, which led to the fruitless duplication of routes throughout Kent. The line opened between Shorncliffe and Barham in 1887 and extended into Canterbury in 1889, but although it linked that centre with Folkestone, it passed through no settlement bigger than the country village of Lyminge and was never a financial success. Passenger trains stopped running north of Lyminge in 1940 and the line closed throughout in 1947.

The Cranbrook & Paddock Wood Railway was authorised to build a line from Paddock Wood to Cranbrook, and in 1882 received powers for an extension to Hawkhurst. Their powers were not exercised, and the railway was eventually built by the South Eastern under Acts of 1887 and 1892 (3D). The line reached Goudhurst (Hope Mill) in 1892 and the terminus at Hawkhurst the following year. Despite occasional bursts of activity during the hopping season, the branch never attracted any substantial traffic and closed throughout in 1961.

Although already guilty of a number of ventures which displayed wild financial misjudgement, the South Eastern reached new heights of absurdity with its scheme for a branch to Chatham Central (2M). To reach the town at all, the South Eastern had to cross the country's widest river and run parallel with the prosperous main line operated by its rival. Its new viaduct across the Medway lay only feet away from the Chatham company's structure, and the line opened to Rochester Common in 1891. Having fought as far as it could into urban Chatham, the line ran out of steam on the outskirts of Rochester – although the South Eastern was not ashamed to give its new and unprepossessing terminus the inappropriate name of Chatham Central when it opened in 1892. The branch did not survive 20 years, closing throughout in 1911.

If the Chatham Central branch was perhaps the South Eastern's most unsound investment, the opening of a new suburban loop line only three years later showed much more foresight. The independent Bexleyheath Railway obtained authorisation for a similar route in 1883, but the powers were amended in 1887 to allow the line to commence just east of Blackheath instead of near Hither Green (5F).

The line opened in 1895 and was worked by the South Eastern from the outset, being absorbed into that company in 1900. Although at the time the line ran through country which was largely undeveloped, the later emergence of North Kent as a suburban stronghold ensured that the loop was to become the thriving and prosperous artery which it remains today.

Two years after the Bexleyheath loop opened, the South Eastern gained a single-track branch to Kingswood in Surrey, which had been promoted by the Chipstead Valley Railway and was absorbed into the South Eastern system in 1899. A year later a second track was laid as far as Tadworth and the original line extended that far. Finally, in 1901, the tracks reached the impressive racecourse station at Tattenham Corner, which was provided with extra platforms to cope with heavy race day traffic.

Meanwhile, in 1892 a loop line opened between Nunhead and Bromley which ran through Catford and provided a valuable relief line for the Chatham company's coast trains. The Shortlands & Nunhead Railway, as it was called (6K), was vested in the Chatham in 1896 and allowed it to use part of the unsuccessful Crystal Palace branch. It was the final Chatham line to be built before amalgamation: after years of competition, the time was growing near when Kent's two great railway companies could join forces in a coalition.

There had been opportunities before, but practical problems and the ongoing bitter rivalry prevented any union. Now, however, the vitality for fighting had been sapped by financial worries, for despite the consistent and heady expansion of both networks, the duplication of routes and wasted resources that resulted from the in-fighting had cost both companies dear.

At last, the two rivals were drawing closer together – and in 1895 they began to share receipts on competitive routes. The decades of dissent were in the past, and in the closing years of the century it gradually became apparent that a new challenge lay ahead – to amalgamate two complex networks of lines and operate the railways of Kent and South London as one body.

The South Eastern & Chatham Joint Committee

The working union between the South Eastern and Chatham companies began on 1 January 1899, when a joint committee took control, although parliamentary sanction for the amalgamation was not received until 5 August. The South Eastern was to receive the larger share of net receipts, 59%, with 41% going to the Chatham. Both companies retained their identities, and each had four representatives sitting on the joint board.

By 1900, the unwieldy title of the SE&LC&DR had been contracted to the South Eastern & Chatham Railway. The amalgamation had not been without its opponents, including many outside interests who felt their personal aims might not be best served by the absence of competition between the two companies. Despite their objections, the union went ahead, and the immediate result was a more efficient and better co-ordinated machine which had total control over the railway traffic throughout a broad and lucrative sector of southern England.

There were, of course, immediate problems to tax the inititative and resolve of the new joint committee. It had inherited a stud of locomotives which contained many underpowered and ageing engines, yet they had to cope with a rapidly increasing level of traffic. Inevitably, serious problems had been created by the years of bitter rivalry, and the operation of the two railways as one entity required a totally different and imaginative approach.

The remoulding of train operations began to take effect with admirable speed. Various simplifications in routing followed the fusion, along with the introduction of new services which made full use of the advantages gained from the amalgamation. In 1901, the only light railway to be worked by the SE&CR opened between Queensborough and Leysdown, although the company was forced to buy a 'Terrier' from the LBSCR to work the line. The Sheppey Light Railway, as it was called, was not formally absorbed into the SE&CR network until 1905 (2G).

Meanwhile, another intrusion had been made into the Brighton company's territory with the opening in 1902 of a branch line from Crowhurst to Bexhill (3F), a line which had been promoted five years earlier under agreement with the South Eastern Railway. At the same time more tracks were laid out of London Bridge, with a new (but short-lived) station at Southwark Park, while the main line was quadrupled as far as Orpington by 1905. The Low Level station at London Bridge had been rebuilt in 1899 and a large new running shed opened at Slades Green. Another new depot near Metropolitan Junction allowed trains to be stabled close to both Cannon Street and Charing Cross and fed quickly into those termini when platforms became free.

In 1901, as already mentioned, the Kingswood branch was extended to its final resting place at Tattenham Corner (4D) and in 1905 the independent Rother Valley Railway, known from 1904 as the Kent & East Sussex Railway, extended its line to link up the SE&CR stations at Headcorn and Robertsbridge (3 xii), although the sparse service on the line gave little incentive to passengers to use it as a through route.

In 1911, improvements at Rochester saw the construction of a new junction between the former South Eastern and Chatham lines, and the complete closure of the now unnecessary branch to Chatham Central. The same year saw the closure of the famous Longhedge locomotive works of the Chatham, following a decision to concentrate activities at Ashford.

A new station at Dover Marine opened in 1915, after the outbreak of war. It was still under construction when the fall of Antwerp in 1914 precipitated its premature use.

The war had come too early to allow the company to complete all its reforms, and the railway's strategic importance and proximity to the heat of the struggle caused numerous and severe problems. At Woolwich, thousands of tons of necessary equipment had to be transported to the ports for use by the army abroad, while a constant stream of materials poured in. The war also saw the running of almost 15,000 special trains conveying men to and from France, while the military mail was dealt with at Victoria and transported via Folkestone.

In 1915 a landslip near Warren Halt necessitated the closure of the Dover-Folkestone line, and the following year saw a catalogue of swingeing economies, with the closure of a number of lines and the temporary suspension of various other sevices which were in some cases never revived.

Dover Town (1G 45) had been closed as a wartime measure in 1914 and its closure was made permanent in 1919. The Queenborough Pier branch closed to passengers in 1914, but services were only restored briefly in 1922 before the branch continued to operate as a freight-only line. The service between Sheerness Dockyard and Sheerness-on-sea (2F) was also suspended between 1914 and 1922.

Passenger trains were suspended between Otford and Sevenoaks (2H) for two years from 1917, and St Leonards Warrior Square (3B 172) closed during the same period. The Bexhill branch (3F) closed completely for 10 months in 1917, although goods trains were restored that year. Passenger trains did not run again until 1919 (to Bexhill), with Sidley re-opening in 1920. Various intermediate stations were closed as an economy measure, including Box Hill (4B 221), Reedham Halt (4D 229) and Smitham (4D 230). The Woodside to Selsdon Road line (4F) closed in 1917 and did not re-open until it was electrified in 1935. Spa Road (5C 274), Southwark Park (5C 275) and Deptford (5C 278) closed for good in 1915, although a new station was constructed at Deptford in 1926. Camberwell (5A 253), Camberwell Gate (5A 254) and Snow Hill (5A 262) all closed permanently to passengers during 1916 and the Greenwich Park branch (6J) closed the following year. The Crystal Palace High Level line (6L) closed between 1917 and 1919, and Battersea Park Road (7A 373), Wandsworth Road (7B 375) and Clapham & North Stockwell (7B 376) lost their passenger services for good in 1916, although the Brighton platforms at the last two stations still remain open.

The war took a heavy toll on the SE&CR. Its rolling stock and locomotives were worn out during the four years of intensive effort, new building in North Kent was throwing up additional traffic burdens on a number of lines, and higher operating costs were making the less successful branches a heavier financial weight round the company's neck. In such circumstances, it was inevitable that when the 1921 Railways Act received Royal Assent for the merging of Britain's railways into four groups of constituent companies, the South Eastern & Chatham was eyed with a certain amount of distaste as one of the less desirable ingredients in what was to shortly become the Southern Railway.

Despite the misgivings, the South Eastern still retained many of the natural advantages that had so inflamed the enthusiasm of the early railway promoters in Kent. In time, and with large-scale electrification, the South Eastern & Chatham system was to prove its worth in the amalgamated system of railway operating that followed the grouping of 1923.

The Southern Railway from 1923

The Southern Railway was authorised by the Railways Act of 1921, but the terms of the amalgamation were to be worked out by the constituent companies, the South Eastern, the London, Chatham & Dover, and the SE&CR Joint Management Committee all being listed as separate entities under the Act. The LBSCR was the first to accept the terms, on 16 November 1922, followed by the London & South Western the following day. Acceptances were received from the South Eastern and Chatham companies on 13 December.

Once the amalgamation had been passed, the Greenwich, the Mid-Kent and the Victoria Station & Pimlico railways, all worked by the SE&CR, were also absorbed. A number of other subsidiary lines, classed with the Brighton and South Western companies, had already been taken in. The three sectors which made up the new Southern Railway were to be called the Western, Central and Eastern divisions, the latter comprising lines formerly operated by the SE&CR.

One immediate result of the grouping was that the two main termini at Victoria and London Bridge now came under the total control of one company – although their diverse and complex histories had resulted in both boasting a total of 12 running lines for dealing with their heavy burdens of traffic – a width of access probably unmatched anywhere in the world.

In 1924 steps were taken to break down the barriers between the Brighton and Chatham stations at Victoria to allow the free access of passengers between the two termini, and by 1926, almost 50 Southern stations had

been reconstructed or improved, and work was in hand for 40 others. Electrification was also proceeding apace, following the inauguration of an enormous electrification programme in 1925. Previously, the Brighton company had pioneered overhead electrification in South London from 1909, but between 1925 and 1939 a large section of the Southern's network was to be converted to third-rail electric operation, work on the first Eastern division lines beginning in 1925 with the Crystal Palace High Level, Holborn Viaduct–Orpington via Nunhead, and Hayes to Elmers End routes. The following year saw the conversion of the main lines out of Charing Cross, Cannon Street and London Bridge, reaching Orpington, Bromley North, Addiscombe, Hayes and Dartford.

1926 also saw the rationalisation of lines in the Ramsgate and Margate area, where competition between the South Eastern and Chatham had resulted in an awkward track layout. A new loop was constructed between Broadstairs on the Chatham line and St Lawrence on the South Eastern to allow through running between Chatham and Ashford, and resulting in the closure of the old Ramsgate stations (1D 30).

Another problem lay in the routeing of through trains from the former Great Northern and Midland lines through Ludgate Hill and London Bridge to Hither Green sidings. The frequency of these trains meant that their running had to be confined to slack operating hours, and it was appreciated that if the old Chatham lines through Elephant & Castle and Nunhead could be utilised, there would be fewer congestion problems on the lines leading to the busy eastern termini. The solution involved the construction of two new loops at Lewisham Junction (6D), which were opened to goods traffic in 1929 and later electrified.

Meanwhile, a new station was opened at Riddlesdown, between Croydon and Oxted, in 1927.

5B365 'Schools' class No 30924 *Haileybury* pauses at Waterloo East with the 11.46 Charing Cross-Ashford on 4 May 1960. *J. Scrace*

The difficult economic conditions of the early 1930s led to the closure of a number of Southern branches, including the oldest constituent of the group, the pioneering Canterbury & Whitstable Railway (1A), in 1931, just over a century after its enthusiastic opening. The Sandgate branch (1H) was curtailed at Hythe the same year. However, the following year saw the opening of the only new line to be constructed in South Eastern & Chatham territory after the grouping, the ill-fated 1¾-mile long branch to Allhallows-on-sea, on the Isle of Grain. It was hoped that this would develop into a thriving seaside resort and dormitory town, but despite the running of through coaches from London for a while, the line never prospered.

At Dover, a new station was opened at Priory, which served the town after the disappearance of the old Chatham station at Dover Harbour in 1927 (1J 61) and the South Eastern one at Dover Town (1G 45) which closed in 1914. The old station at Admiralty Pier, meanwhile, had been rebuilt as Dover Marine during the war, and acted as a transfer station for Continental passengers.

1934 saw the building of a modern locomotive and carriage depot at Stewarts Lane, Battersea, where prior to amalgamation, the old Chatham works at Longhedge had been entirely separate from the neighbouring depot of the Brighton company.

Out in the Romney Marshes, a new line was constructed to make it easier to work the two short branches from Lydd to New Romney and Dungeness. The short linking line, known as the Greatstone Deviation, ran parallel with the coast and had the added advantage of tapping some of the holiday traffic generated by the diminutive narrow-gauge Romney, Hythe & Dymchurch Railway. The line opened in 1937, and the section of track leading to the former terminus at Dungeness was abandoned at the same time.

The advent of World War 2 meant the shelving of the Southern's electrification plans and the temporary closure of a number of stations and the halting of progress on a number of other projects. The drama of the war years is adequately described elsewhere (cf *Bibliography*) as is the fascinating period of electrification and stock modernisation which followed the war.

For the purposes of this book, the old South Eastern & Chatham network suffered little as a direct result of the war – although the Elham Valley line closed throughout to passengers in 1947 (the northern section having closed in 1940) and the Sheppey Light Railway (2G) closed throughout in 1950. The remaining section of the Sandgate branch (1H), from Sandling Junction to Hythe, closed in 1951.

But it was in 1947 that the Transport Act was passed, requiring the nationalisation of all major railways. It became effective on 1 January 1948, and by the 16th of that month the first engine in the new BR colours – then a temporary design with the number prefaced by the letter S – was sent to Waterloo for official inspection.

During its 24-year lifespan, the Southern Railway had successfully catered for the boom in suburban housing which took place in the 1930s and had introduced widespread electrification, modernised track layouts and reformed the signalling system. Its last years were clouded by the confusion that followed World War 2, but it had never suffered the degradations that affected the industrial parts of Britain during the slump years. Its legacy to British Railways – as the new nationalised system was to become – was an extremely efficient network of lines which capitalised on the natural advantages offered by the high density of population in the south, the proximity of the Continent and a local economy that relied on commuter and holiday traffic – along with income generated from flowers, fruit and hop-growing.

Nationalisation

With the election in 1945 of a strong Labour government, the nationalisation of Britain's railways threatened during the war became a certainty. The proclaimed objective was state control and

3D189 'H' Class 0-4-4T No 31543 stands at Hawkhurst on 27 May 1961 after working in with the 12.30 from Paddock Wood. *J. Scrace*

co-ordination of all public transport, and the 1947 Transport Act contained powers for the establishment of an all-encompassing British Transport Commission, within which separate executives were charged with the everyday management of the main-line railways, roads, docks, canals and London Transport.

The first general manager of the whole of British Railways was Sir Eustace Missenden, formerly of the Southern and South Eastern & Chatham railways. A man experienced in the smallest of the grouped companies, where the personal touch was still strong, he was keen to see the new national railway company creating a favourable impression with passengers, and encouraged staff to take a pride in their job.

The Southern escaped the operating changes imposed on the larger of the pre-nationalisation companies, and was transformed, almost lock, stock and barrel, into the new Southern Region of British Railways.

The most momentous decision made by the Railway Executive was to persist with steam traction and invest in a new range of standard engines, despite the rapid progress that had been made with dieselisation abroad. No other railway in the progressive western world made such a heavy commitment to steam in the postwar period – and it was as a result of this investment that British Railways was subsequently forced into the most hectic modernisation programme ever attempted.

In the first years after the 1948 nationalisation, there was little spare money to be spent, with the country still recovering from the post war recession.

The Tories' 1953 Transport Act abolished the BTC's executives, including the Railway Executive, and as a direct result the stature and power of the regional managers was greatly increased. Then in 1955 came plans for a massive modernisation and reinvestment programme that was to change the face of Britain's railways. The injection of cash was to allow for widespread dieselisation and selective electrification, the reconstruction of track and the building of new rolling stock. In the southeast, Cannon Street station had been rebuilt following war damage, and extensive drainage and coastal defence work carried out at the Warren.

Now there was scope for the long-awaited mainline electrification to take place. A handful of diesel-electric locomotives were turned out at Ashford in 1951 and tested all over the country, performing with some success on the Kent express trains, the 'Golden Arrow' and the 'Night Ferry'.

Then the decision was made to progressively withdraw steam traction from the Eastern Section of the Southern Region, and electrification – as planned before the outbreak of war – could at last be undertaken. Diesel electrification was completed to Hastings via Tunbridge Wells in 1957, and a major Kent Coast third-rail electrification scheme was given the go-ahead by the British Transport Commission the previous year.

The first stage came to fruition in 1959, when electric public services were introduced between London, Ramsgate and Dover via Faversham. The entire track layout between Shortlands Junction and Bickley Junction was reorganised and the four-track main line extended from Bickley Junction through St Mary Cray to Swanley. St Mary Cray was completely rebuilt and the platforms at Chatham extended to accommodate 12-car trains, with slow lines and sidings taken out and new tracks laid for 2¼ miles between Rainham and Newington. On the Sheerness branch, the single line was doubled between Sittingbourne Middle Junction and a point south of Swale Halt to allow more track capacity for a new service of multiple-unit trains.

In all, around 35 stations were altered to provide extra space for 12-car trains, and colour-light signalling and track circuitry was installed throughout from Victoria to Ramsgate and on the Catford Loop. The only regular passenger service on the newly-electrified line not to be operated by multiple-units was the 'Night Ferry', run by new electric locomotives. The 'Golden Arrow' and other boat trains continued to be steam operated via Tonbridge and Ashford. The full electric service on the former South Eastern lines in Kent, excluding the Ashford-Hastings run, came into operation in 1962 as the final stage of the scheme.

Meanwhile there was a growing concern in parliament at the financial crisis that was now facing the railways: early teething troubles with the new forms of traction had frustrated all hopes of reversing BR's economic decline in the late 1950s, and by early 1960 Harold Macmillan's Conservative government had decided a new managerial approach was essential. An advisory group of industrialists was set up to recommend how the railways' future should be shaped, and the product of their research was a new form of management – in the form of the British Railways Board, established under the 1963 Transport Act. The man at the helm on the new board – and the one who presided over the dissolution of the old British Transport Commission – was a leading industrialist whose name was to become one of the most famous – or notorious – in recent railway history, Dr Richard (later Lord) Beeching. He became chairman of a board which had substantial freedoms to pick and choose the traffic it would carry. Another crucial change was that the government now shouldered the responsibility for deciding whether loss-making services should be scrapped. The BRB could propose any line for closure, and the case would then be submitted to a new Transport Users' Consultative Committee for investigation, with the final verdict lying with the Ministry of Transport.

Lord Beeching spent only a short time 'on the railways' – arriving from ICI in 1963 and returning there in 1965 – but he was the guiding force behind a document which appalled the country when it appeared in the spring of 1963 – a 'Reshaping Report' which immediately became known as the Beeching Plan. It advocated closure of over 5,000 route miles of railway and 2,350 stations – and the rationalisation programme also included major cuts in manpower and signalled the end of steam.

Compared with other parts of the country, the South Eastern lines escaped relatively unscathed from the era of the Beeching axe, although many stations lost their goods facilities and a number of less profitable intermediate halts were closed. 1961 was in fact the worst year for the Kent branch lines, witnessing the closure of the Isle of Grain line from Hoo Junction to passengers, and the complete closure of the Allhallows

13

light railway, the Hawkhurst and Westerham branches, and the final section of the Kent & East Sussex line between Tenterden and Robersbridge, which had closed to passengers in 1954. The Bexhill branch followed in 1964 and the Dungeness and New Romney lines in 1967.

The 1968 Transport Act brought more crucial changes nationwide, including the introduction of the first passenger transport executives aimed at integrating rail and bus services, and the introduction of line-by-line financial support for routes considered to be socially necessary. The 1974 Act reshaped this financial support in the form of a global Public Service Obligation grant, under which the entire passenger system received a central fund of finance.

In the southeast, the pattern of operations stabilised with widespread electrification. In the past 20 years there have been few major closures and successive track reconstruction and signalling schemes have improved the reliability of services on the most intensive routes. For many commuters there have been few obvious or momentous changes, with many services still relying on on early multiple-unit stock which has been occasionally refurbished over the years.

The most noticeable changes came with the decision to alter the Southern Region's green coaching stock livery to bring it into line with the blue and grey standard identity of British Rail in the 1970s, and the resigning and modernisation of stations. Gradually, brand new electric multiple-units have been brought into use since 1979 to replace the most outdated stock. But as well as fighting for its fair share of all the latest developments in modern railway operation, the South Eastern network also provides a strong base for preservation activities.

Beside the Kent/Sussex border there has been a revival of part of one of the atmospheric Colonel Stephens' lines, the Kent & East Sussex, while in the depths of the Romney marshes the unique 15in gauge Romney, Hythe & Dymchurch Railway is as popular as ever with holidaymakers and schoolchildren. Kent's paper-making industry has not been forgotten either, with the revitalisation of the Sittingbourne & Kemsley

Light Railway, mid-way between Gillingham and Faversham.

For more than a century, the southeast witnessed the full glory of the reign of steam, from the early primitive locomotives to the great giants of the Southern Railway and the impressive standard engines of BR days.

Across the years, and under successive managements, the lines retained much of their unique character and identity and in many places, the countryside itself remains largely unchanged today. The steam trains may have gone – and with them many of the more lethargic branch lines – but the passengers of the 1980s can still look out on the small neat villages, rolling fields and hedge-lined roads that have witnessed decades of passing boat trains and pullmans, hop-pickers' specials and holiday excursions.

Today, the south eastern system forms the basis of a thriving and prosperous electrified network, with tightly-crammed commuter trains serving the London suburbs and the dormitory towns of North Kent. Express trains to the coast still whip excited passengers along the first stage of their journey to the Continent, and the old resorts are also thriving: Margate, Ramsgate, Herne Bay and Broadstairs, names that became famous with generations of holidaymakers and day-trippers.

Off the beaten track, the rambler can still find traces of the past on weed-covered platforms and long-empty track beds. The lost termini of central London, the branch lines to Westerham, Hawkhurst, Port Victoria and Sandgate, the light railways from Shepherds Well and Rolvenden: much of the South Eastern's history can still be traced from empty bay platforms over disused bridges and embankments to rusting rails on deserted quays. For the regular traveller and historian alike, Kent's railway heritage is kept alive alongside the prosperous lines that carry the fast electric trains of the eighties. And for the enthusiast who searches hard enough, the vital clues still remain to an era when Lord Beeching was unheard of and when the great steam expresses roared confidently through the south of England.

1

Canterbury, Dover and Thanet

Contents

Appendix
1. East Kent (Light) Railway

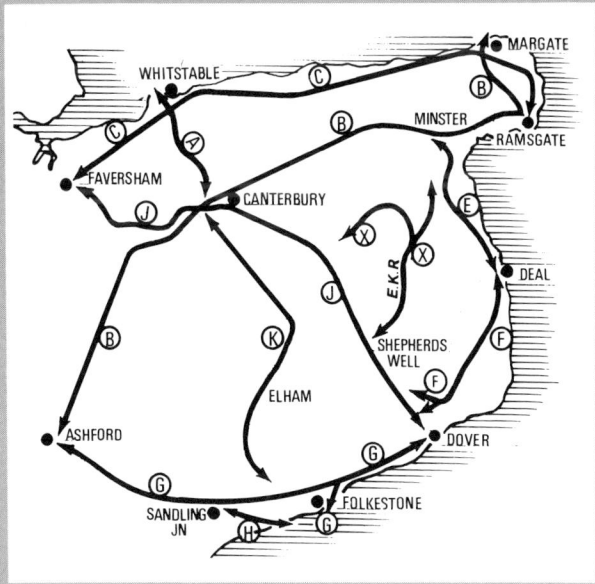

A

Canterbury & Whitstable Railway

The Company
Incorporated 1825
Leased to the SER 29/09/1844
Sold to the SER 13/12/1853

Opening Dates
Canterbury (C&W)–Whitstable (C&W)
ceremonial 03/05/1830
public 04/05/1830
Whitstable Harbour branch 19/03/1832
Canterbury (C&W)–Canterbury (SER) 06/04/1846[a]

Closure Dates
Canterbury–Whitstable P 01/01/31
Canterbury–Whitstable G/CC 01/03/53[b]

Lines Remaining Open
None

Remarks
a: Loop line opened to new SER station and trains
diverted from C&W station
b: Line was originally closed completely on 01/12/52
but re-opened on 05/02/53 when floods damaged
Kent Coast line

No	Station (original name)		Opened	Closed to passengers	Closed to goods	Closed completely
1	Canterbury*	(C+W station)	03/05/1830 (c) 04/05/1830 (p)	06/04/1846	CDO 06/04/1846	1848
2	Blean & Tyler Hill Halt*®		—/01/08	01/01/31	—	01/01/31
3	South Street Halt		01/06/11	01/01/31	—	01/01/31
4	Tankerton Halt		—/07/14	01/01/31	—	01/01/31
5	Whitstable	(C+W station)	03/05/1830 (c) 04/05/1830 (p)	—/03/1846	unaffected	see entry below
6	Whitstable	(2nd station)	—/03/1846	—/02/1894	unaffected	see entry below
7	Whitstable*®	(3rd station)	—/02/1894	01/01/31	01/03/53	01/03/53

Notes to table
1 Station closed to passengers when loop line
opened to SER station in 1846 and trains were
diverted. It continued as a coal depot, possibly
until 1848. Some sources give the station's final
closure date as being around 1900

2 ® Tyler Hill Halt —/05/12(t)
  ® Blean & Tyler Hill Halt —/12/15(t)
7 ® Whitstable Harbour 01/07/1899
Whistable Harbour branch opened 19/03/1832. It
was originally closed completely 01/12/52, but RO
05/02/53 when floods damaged the Kent Coast line

B

SER, Canterbury–Thanet branch

The Company
South Eastern Railway[a]

Opening Dates
Ashford–Canterbury 06/02/1846
Canterbury–Ramsgate 13/04/1846
Ramsgate (Town)–Margate (Sands) 01/12/1846
St Lawrence Loop —/07/1863

Closure Date
Ramsgate Town–Margate Sands P/G/CC 02/07/26[b]

Lines Remaining Open
Ashford–Canterbury – Ramsgate (new station)[b]
Pass/Goods

Remarks
a: Notes on SER contained in introduction
b: The branch to Margate and station at Ramsgate
Town were closed when the line was extended
through Ramsgate towards the coast and a new
station erected to serve Ramsgate

8	Wye	06/02/1846	Wye	10/06/63	P
9	Chilham*	06/02/1846	Chilham	15/08/66	P
10	Chartham*	—/—/1859	Chartham	19/11/62	P
11	Canterbury*®	06/02/1846	Canterbury West	†	P/G
12	Sturry*	01/06/1847	Sturry	01/05/62	P
12a	Chislet Colliery*®	N/A	04/10/71	—	04/10/71
13	Grove Ferry*®	13/04/1846	03/01/66	30/04/60	03/01/66
14	Minster*®	13/04/1846	Minster	09/09/63	P
14a	Ebbsfleet & Cliffsend Halt	—/05/08	01/04/33	—	01/04/33
15	St Lawrence (Pegwell Bay)	—/10/1864	03/04/16	—	03/04/16
16	Ramsgate*®	13/04/1846	02/07/26	02/07/26	02/07/26
17	Margate*®	01/12/1846	02/07/26	20/12/26	20/12/26

Notes to table
9 Unstaffed from 14/04/69
10 Unstaffed from 14/04/69. Chartham Siding G/CC 06/03/61
11 ® Canterbury (West) 01/07/1899. Coal depot closed 1984. Freight depot, oil terminal remain
12 G 01/05/62 except private sidings since closed
12a ® Chislet Colliery Halt 05/05/69
13 ® Grove Ferry & Upstreet 20/09/54
14 ® Minster Junction 01/01/1852; ® Minster Junction (Thanet) 01/08/01; ® Minster (Thanet)

07/05/45; ® Minster, probably 1971/2; G 09/09/63 except private sidings since closed
16 ® Ramsgate Town 01/07/1899. Closed completely with opening of new line 02/07/26 and replaced by new station Ramsgate (cf. 1D)
17 ® Margate Sands 01/07/1899. Line to Ramsgate closed completely with opening of new line 02/07/26, except for short goods siding on the old line, which was accessible from Margate West and closed completely 20/12/26

1B8 The level crossing and main station buildings at Wye in British Railways days. The station dates from the opening of the line to Canterbury in 1846, and the Tudor style red brick buildings are on the Down side of the line.

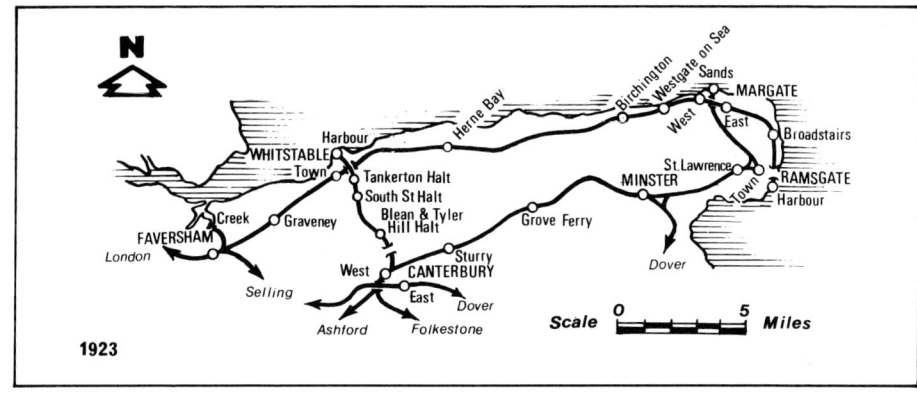

1923

C

Herne Bay & Faversham Railway

The Company
Incorporated 1857
® Margate & London Railway 1859
® Kent Coast Railway 1861
Sold to the LCDR 1871

Opening Dates
Faversham Creek branch 12/04/1860
Faversham–Whitstable Town 01/08/1860
Whitstable Town–Herne Bay 13/07/1861
Herne Bay–Margate – Ramsgate 05/10/1863

Closure Date
Ramsgate Harbour, terminus and old line P/G/CC
02/07/26[a]

Lines Remaining Open
Faversham Docks (freight only)
Faversham–Ramsgate (new station) Pass/Goods

Remarks
a: Closed with opening of new line, see map

18	Graveney Siding*	N/A	—	05/02/62	05/02/62
19	Whitstable Town*®	01/08/1860	01/01/15	unaffected	see entry below
20	Whitstable Town*® (2nd station)	01/01/15	Whitstable	18/04/64	P
21	Chestfield & Swalecliffe Halt*®	06/07/30	Chestfield & Swalecliffe	—	P
22	Herne Bay & Hampton-on-Sea*®	13/07/1861	Herne Bay	CDO 16/10/65 07/10/68	P
23	Birchington*®	05/10/1863	Birchington-on-Sea	04/06/62	P
24	Westgate-on-Sea	—/04/1871	Westgate-on-Sea	06/11/61	P
25	Margate*®	05/10/1863	Margate	01/11/72	P
26	East Margate*®	—/—/1870	04/05/53	—	04/05/53
27	Broadstairs*	05/10/1863	Broadstairs	03/06/63	P
28	Ramsgate*®	05/10/1863	02/07/26	02/07/26	02/07/26

Notes to table
18 No passenger facilities. Marked on various maps as simply Graveney
19 ® Whitstable-on-Sea —/07/1879 (t)
    ® Whitstable Town 01/07/1899 ® Whitstable, probably early 1979
20 ® Whitstable & Tankerton 01/02/36
21 ® Chestfield & Swalecliffe
22 ® Herne Bay —/03/51 G 07/10/68 except private sidings which have since closed
23 ® Birchington-on-Sea —/10/1878 (t)

25 ⓡ Margate & Cliftonville —–/12/1880 (t)
    ⓡ Margate West 01/07/1899
    ⓡ Margate 11/07/26
26 ⓡ Margate East 01/07/1899
27 G 03/06/63 except private sidings since closed
28 ⓡ Ramsgate & St Lawrence-on-Sea —/06/1871
    ⓡ Ramsgate Harbour 01/07/1899
    Closed completely when new line opened 02/07/26.
    New line ran from 2m 52ch from Broadstairs to 3m
    74ch from Minster (via new Ramsgate station). It
    was 1m 48ch long

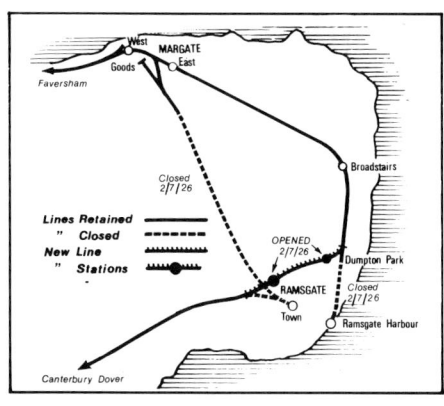

**1C22 Class L 4-4-0 No 31779 climbs out of Herne Bay
with a down Ramsgate train in August 1958.**
Brian Coates

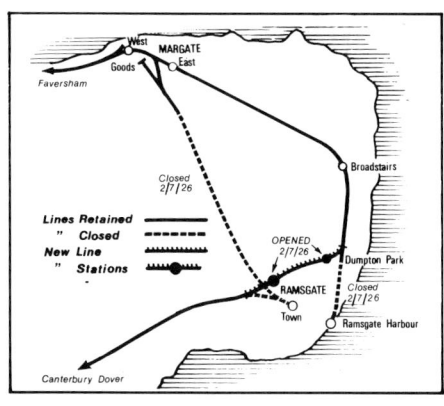

Below:
1C23 An LC&DR 2-4-0 engine stands at the Down platform, Birchington-on-sea, in the early years of this century. Note the combined waiting room and shelter and the large nameboards. The station, built in 1863, was plain Birchington until around 1878.

Bottom:
1C28 Holiday crowds at Ramsgate, with the distinctive overall roof of the former LC&DR Harbour station in the background. The station closed in 1926 with the opening of a new line and station.

Right:
IC28 Another view of Ramsgate Harbour station, showing the turntable at the platform-end. The station opened in 1863 with the line from Herne Bay.

D

SR, Ramsgate and Minster loops

The Company
Southern Railway[a]

Opening Dates
Ramsgate Loop
(Broadstairs (jn)–St Lawrence (jn): 02/07/26[b],[c]
Minster Loop: 07/07/29[b]

Closure Date
None

Lines Remaining Open
Both loops, to passenger and freight

Remarks
a: see introduction
b: see maps
c: Ramsgate loop now forms part of main line between
   Broadstairs and Minster

29	Dumpton Park*®	02/07/26		Dumpton Park	—	P
30	Ramsgate*	02/07/26		Ramsgate	†	P/G

Notes to table
29 ® Dumpton Park (for East Ramsgate) 12/03/27
    ® Dumpton Park
30 Second, resited station, opened with new line.
    Open to passengers and freight (train-load traffic
    only). Carriage sidings and Ramsgate (RE) EMU
    depot.

1D30 Line-up of electric stock at Ramsgate EMU
depot in June, 1975. 2-HAP No 6082 stands alongside
4-CEP No 7192, 4-VEP No 7881 and a rake of Midland
Region Mark I coaches. The steam shed at Ramsgate,
coded 74B, and 73G from 1958, closed in 1962.
Keith Dungate

E

SER, Deal branch

The Company
South Eastern Railway[a]

Opening Date
Minster–Deal 01/07/1847

Closure Date
None

Line Remaining Open
Minster–Deal Pass/Goods

Remarks
a: see introduction

30a	Richborough Castle Halt*	19/06/33	11/09/39	—†	11/09/39
31	Sandwich	01/07/1847	Sandwich	07/10/63	P
32	Deal*	01/07/1847	Deal	01/05/72†	P

Notes to table
30a 19/06/33 was public opening date. The station was open for military use from 29/06/18. Richborough CEGB Power Station located south of Minster

32 Betteshanger Colliery located north of Deal

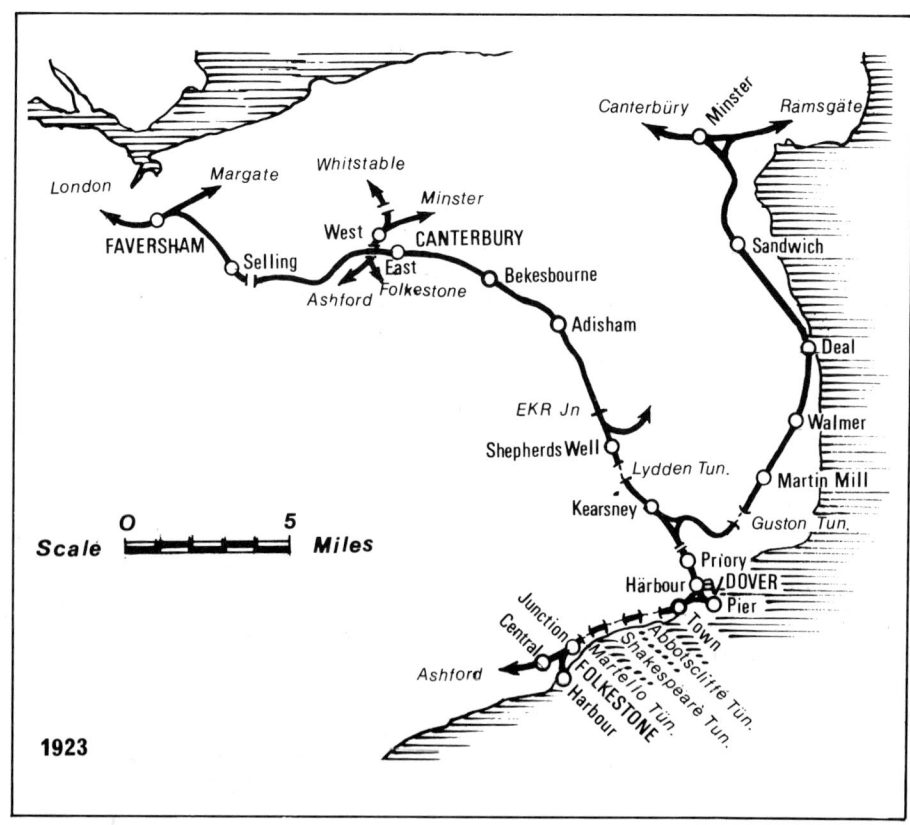

1923

F

Deal & Dover Railway

The Company
Incorporated 1865
Agreement for joint railway, run as Deal Joint Railway
1874[a]

Opening Dates
Deal–Dover(Buckland Jn) 15/06/1881
LCDR Kearsney loop 01/07/1882

Closure Date
Kearsney loop P/G/CC 08/08/72

Line Remaining Open
Deal–Dover (Buckland Jn) Pass/Goods

Remarks
a: Joint railway run by SER and LCDR

| 33 | Walmer | 15/06/1881 | Walmer | 02/10/61 | P |
| 34 | Martin Mill* | 15/06/1881 | Martin Mill | 04/09/61 | P |

Note to table
34 Last passenger train over Kearsney loop was 'Man of Kent' special, 11/04/71. Last goods train over loop was Fisons weedkilling train 19/06/72. The

Kearsney loop eliminated reversals at Priory. Loop completely closed, 08/08/72

1F33 The Up platform at Walmer, on the Deal Joint Railway. The station buildings date from 1881, when the line opened between Deal and Dover.

G

SER, Ashford–Dover line

The Company
South Eastern Railway[a]

Opening Dates
Ashford–Folkestone (temporary station) 28/06/1843
Folkestone (temporary)–Folkestone (permanent station) 18/12/1843[b]
Folkestone–Dover 07/02/1844[c]
Folkestone Harbour branch (Goods) 1843
Folkestone Harbour branch (Pass) 01/01/1849

Closure Date
Folkstone Harbour branch G 17/08/68

Line Remaining Open
Ashford–Dover Pass/Goods
Folkestone Harbour branch Pass

Remarks
a: see introduction
b: temporary station closed when line extended to permanent station
c: This station at Dover was renamed Dover Town in 1861 temporarily closed as a wartime measure on 14/10/14 and permanently closed 11/08/19

No.	Station		Opening			
35	Smeeth		—/10/1852	04/01/54	18/04/64	18/04/64
36	Westenhanger & Hythe*®		07/02/1844	Westenhanger 25/03/63		P
37	Sandling Junction*®		01/01/1888	Sandling 04/02/63		P
38	Cheriton Halt*		01/05/08	16/06/47	—	16/06/47
39	Shorncliffe Camp (1st)*®		01/11/1863	01/02/1881	unaffected	see entry below
40	Shorncliffe Camp (2nd)*®		01/02/1881	Folkestone West CDO 26/04/65 22/04/68		P
41	Folkestone	(temp. station)	28/06/1843	18/12/1843	18/12/1843	18/12/1843
42	Cheriton Arch*®		01/09/1884	Folkestone Central	—	P
43	Folkestone*®		18/12/1843	06/09/65	†	G
44	Warren Halt*®		01/06/08	25/09/39	—	†
45	Dover*®		07/02/1844	14/10/14	11/08/19	11/08/19
46	Folkestone Harbour (1st)		01/01/1849	—/—/1850	unaffected	see entry below
47	Folkestone Harbour (2nd)*		—/—/1850	Folkestone Harbour 17/08/68		P

Notes to table

36 ® Westenhanger 01/10/1874. Unstaffed station from 01/02/71, except on race days at nearby Folkestone racecourse – original racecourse platforms now disused

37 ® Sandling 03/12/51

38 TC 01/12/15, RO 14/06/20; TC 01/02/41–07/10/46

39 ® Shorncliffe & Sandgate 01/12/1863; ® Shorncliffe Camp 01/10/1874

40 ® Shorncliffe 02/07/26; ® Folkestone West 10/09/62

42 ® Radnor Park —/09/1886; ® Folkestone Central 01/06/1895

43 The permanent station at Folkestone appears to have been known by a wide variety of different names, according to timetables and other sources. A selection are given, but not all will have been carried on station nameboards or on official maps. Folkestone (also initially known as Folkstone); Folkestone Old —/07/1849t; Folkestone Junction —/01/1852; Folkestone Junction (Shorncliffe) —/09/1858; Folkestone Junction —/11/1863; Folkestone —/04/1884; Folkestone Junction —/06/1897; ® Folkestone East 10/09/62. Goods sidings in occasional use, carriage sidings. Staff halt remains at Folkestone East, but without signboards

44 P/CC 25/09/39 temporarily and closure made permanent 1951-2. RO as Folkestone Warren, excursion station. Remains in use as Folkestone Warren Staff Halt for staff working on sea defences. There was another tiny halt constructed between Warren Halt and Dover, known as Shakespeare Cliff Halt, or Shakespeare Halt. The halt opened on 2/6/13 for mining use, and was later used by the navy and military. It remains in use as Shakespeare Cliff Staff Halt, serving the Channel tunnel workings. A siding behind the halt can be worked from Archcliffe Junction signalbox

45 ® Dover Town —/12/1861t. (Dover Bulwark St. oil terminal west of Archcliffe Jn) TC 12/01/1877–12/03/1877 (landslip). TC 14/10/14, made permanent 11/08/19

47 Station TC 29/11/15–01/03/19

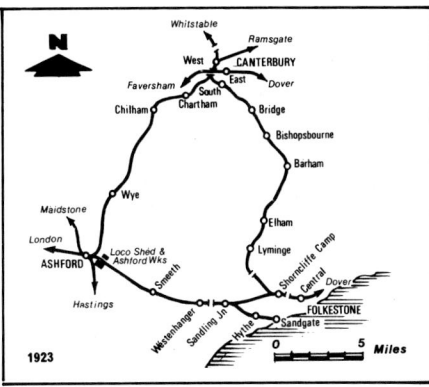

Below:
1G36 Station staff almost outnumber passengers in this period shot of Westenhanger station, opened by the SER as Westenhanger and Hythe in 1844.

Bottom:
1G37 A branch line train at Sandling Junction in 1891, three years after the station opened. The main line opened in 1843 and the branch itself in 1874 – although services were cut back to Hythe in 1931 and the line closed completely in 1951.

Top left:
1G42 Radnor Park station in 1890, six years after opening as Cheriton Arch. It became Folkestone Central in 1895.

Centre left:
1G43 The permanent SER station at Folkestone was known by a variety of names, but became Folkestone Junction in 1897 and Folkestone East in 1962. Opened in 1843, it closed to passengers in 1965, but a staff halt remains.

Bottom left:
1G44a Shakespeare halt was a tiny unstaffed station located amid the chalk cliffs between Folkestone and Dover.

Top:
1G47 The footbridge and canopies form intricate shapes at Folkestone Harbour station in this early picture. Passenger trains began running on the branch in 1849 and the permanent station was completed the following year.

Above:
1G47 The 1.05pm blasts up the bank outside Folkestone Harbour station on 17 September 1955.

27

H

SER, Sandgate branch

The Company
South Eastern Railway[a]

Opening Date
Sandling Junction–Sandgate
  ceremonial 09/10/1874
  public 10/10/1874

Closure Dates
Hythe–Sandgate P/G/CC 01/04/31
Sandling Jn–Hythe P/G/CC 03/12/51[b]

Lines Remaining Open
None

Remarks
a: see introduction
b: this section temporarily closed 03/05/43, RO 01/10/45

48	Hythe*®	10/10/1874	03/12/51	03/12/51	03/12/51
49	Sandgate*	10/10/1874	01/04/31	01/04/31	01/04/31

Notes to table
48 ® Hythe (Kent) 21/09/25; ® Hythe for Sandgate —/11/31; ® Hythe 02/07/39.

Ceremonial opening 09/10/1874. TC 03/05/43–01/10/45.
49 Ceremonial opening 09/10/1874.

J

East Kent Railway (Eastern Section)

The Company
Incorporated 1853[a]
® London, Chatham & Dover Railway 01/08/1859

Opening Dates
Faversham–Canterbury 09/07/1860
Canterbury–Dover Town 22/07/1861[b]
Dover Town–Dover Harbour 01/11/1861[b]
Admiralty Pier branch 30/08/1864

Closure Dates
None

Line Remaining Open
Faversham–Dover Western Docks Pass/Goods

Remarks
a: cf section 2D for Western Section, Bickley–Faversham.
b: the station opened as Dover Town in 1861 was renamed Dover Priory in 1863

50	Selling		03/12/1860	Selling	05/11/62	P
51	Canterbury*®		09/07/1860	Canterbury East	13/09/65	P
52	Bekesbourne*		22/07/1861	Bekesbourne	05/06/61	P
53	Adisham*		22/07/1861	Adisham	07/05/62†	P
54	Aylesham Halt*		01/07/28	Aylesham	—	P
55	Snowdown Halt*®		—/—/1914	Snowdown	—	P
56	Shepherd's Well*		22/07/1861	Shepherd's Well	10/06/63†	P
57	Stonehall & Lydden Halt		—/—/1914		05/04/54	—	05/04/54
58	Ewell*®		01/08/1862	Kearsney	04/09/61	P
59	Dover Town*®		22/07/1861	Dover Priory	03/07/61	P
60	Dover Harbour (1st)*		01/11/1861	—/06/1863t	unaffected	see entry below
61	Dover Town & Harbour*®		—/06/1863t		10/07/27	†	10/07/27
61a	Dover Bulwark Street*		N/A		—	15/08/66†	15/08/66
62	Dover (Admiralty Pier)*®		30/08/1864	—/08/14	unaffected	see entry below
63	Dover Marine*®	(military)	02/01/15	Dover Western Docks	†	P/G
		(public)	18/01/19			

Notes to table

51 ® Canterbury East 01/07/1899
52 Unstaffed from 14/04/69
53 Closed to goods except private sidings traffic
54 ® Aylesham and rebuilt c1960
55 ® Snowdown & Nonnington Halt; ® Snowdown & Nonnington; ® Snowdown, —/06/80; Unstaffed from 14/04/69. Branch to Snowdown Colliery, south of station, east side of line, since closed
56 Branch to Tilmanstone Colliery, north of station, east side of line
58 ® Kearsney 01/02/1869
59 Possibly known as Dover Town (Priory). ® Dover

Priory —/07/1863t; Branch to train ferry from Hawkesbury Street Jn, south of station
60 Original terminus on spur, south of 2nd station
61 Resited station. ® Dover Harbour 01/07/1899 see note 63 for goods services
61a Closed to goods except BP oil depot
62 ® Dover Marine 05/12/18. See official opening dates in table
63 ® Western Docks 14/05/79. Goods include Town Yard (marshalling), Western Docks carriage shed, Ferry sidings and car unloading facilities on the military dock

Above:
1J51 The LC&DR opened their station at Canterbury and the line to Faversham in 1860. It was extended to Dover the following year. The station was renamed Canterbury East in 1899 and this picture in BR days shows the original overall roof still standing.

Right:
1J51 A train to Dover Marine departs from Canterbury East beneath the elegant 1926 signals and impressive signal box in October, 1977, formed of a solitary Class 423 4-VEP unit, No 7855.
Quentin Williamson

Above:
1J51   Class 423 4-VEP unit No 7769 leaves Canterbury East bound for Dover Marine in June 1980.
Quentin Williamson

Left:
1J55   The bare wooden platforms of Snowdown and Nonnington Halt, sporting Southern Region totems. The halt was opened in 1914.

Below left:
1J63   A continental flavour at Dover Marine, opened to passengers in 1919 and replacing the Admiralty Pier station of 1864.

K

Elham Valley Light Railway

The Company
Incorporated 1881
Sold to SER 1884

Closure Dates
Harbledown Jn–Lyminge P 01/12/40
Lyminge–Shorncliffe (jn) P 16/06/47[a]
Harbledown Jn–Shorncliffe (jn) G/CC 01/10/47

Lines Remaining Open
None

Opening Dates
Harbledown Junction–Barham 01/07/1889
Barham–Shorncliffe (jn) 04/07/1887

Remarks
a: this section closed 03/05/43, RO 07/10/46

64	South Canterbury*®	01/07/1889	01/12/40	01/10/47	01/10/47
65	Bridge	01/07/1889	01/12/40	01/10/47	01/10/47
66	Bishopsbourne	01/07/1889	01/12/40	01/10/47	01/10/47
67	Barham	04/07/1887	01/12/40	01/10/47	01/10/47
68	Elham	04/07/1887	01/12/40	01/10/47	01/10/47
69	Lyminge*	04/07/1887	16/06/47	01/10/47	01/10/47

Notes to table
64 ® Canterbury South. (Clinker does not record the station as being named South Canterbury)
69 TC 03/05/43–07/10/46

1K69 A rural scene on the Elham Valley Light Railway. Lyminge opened with the first section of the line in 1887 and was the last to retain passenger services, closing in 1947.

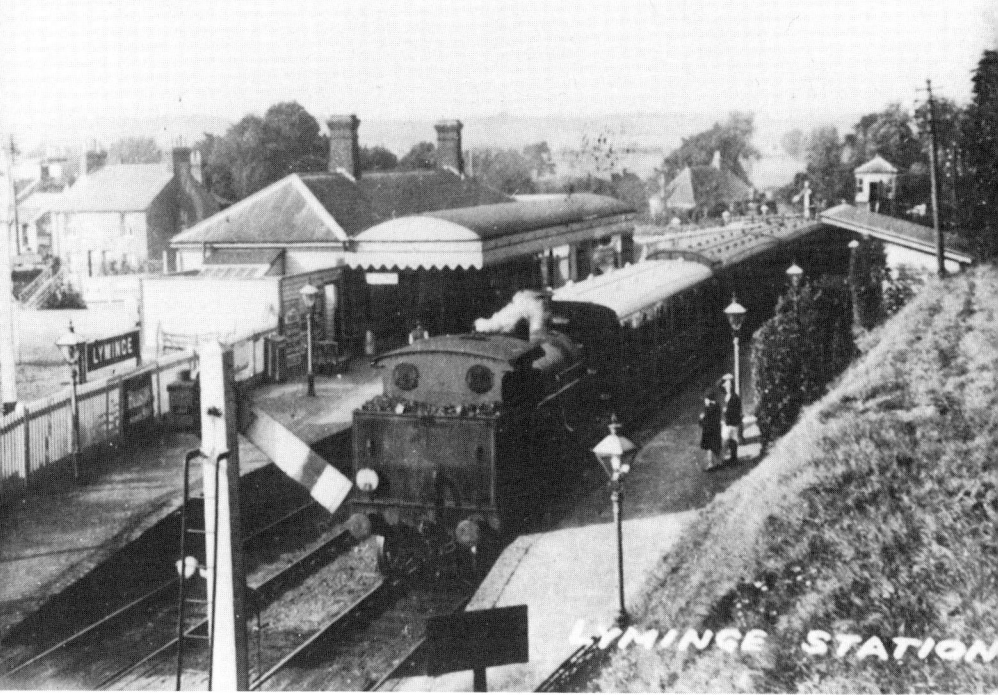

Appendix One:
East Kent (Light) Railway

The Company
The East Kent Railway was one of a number of independent lines operated by Colonel H. F. Stephens from his offices in Tonbridge. A light railway order was granted on 19/06/11

Opening Dates
Shepherd's Well–Wingham Colliery
   O (goods) November 1912
   Inaugural train 27/11/12
   O (pass) 16/10/16
Eastry–Sandwich Road O (p&g) 1925
Sandwich Rd–Richborough O (goods) 1925[a]
Wingham Colliery–Canterbury Rd O (p&g) 1925

Closure Dates
Eastry–Sandwich Road P 01/11/28[a]
Canterbury Rd–Shepherd's Well P 01/11/48
Eastry–Richborough G/CC 27/10/49[b]

Eastry–Canterbury Road G/CC 25/07/50
Eastry–Eythorne G/CC 01/07/51

Line Remaining Open
Shepherd's Well–Tilmanstone Colliery   Goods[c]

Remarks
a: No passenger traffic beyond Sandwich Road
b: Sandwich Rd–Richborough section lay derelict from 1939
c: Main goods services withdrawn from Tilmanstone on 08/08/64

Stations
The stations were much less substantial than those on the main lines, and were primitive even by Col Stephens' standards, most boasting only wooden buildings without light or running water.

	Open	Closed	Notes
On the Richborough branch were:			
Richborough (goods only)	1925	1949	a
Sandwich Road	1925	P 1928	
Roman Road	1925	P 1928	b
Poison Cross	1925	P 1928	c
On the main line:			
Shepherd's Well (EKR station)	1916	P 1948	
Eythorne	1916	P 1948	
Tilmanstone Colliery Halt	1916	P 1948	
Elvington	1925	P 1948	d
Knowlton Halt	1916	P 1948	
Eastry South	1925	P 1948	
Eastry	1916	P 1948	
Woodnesborough	1925	P 1948	e
Ash Town	1916	P 1948	
Staple	1916	P 1948	
Wingham Colliery Halt	1916	P 1948	
Wingham Town	1925	P 1948	
Wingham, Canterbury Road	1925	P 1948	f

Notes
a: Derelict from 1939
b: Roman Road, Woodnesborough was
   (R) Woodnesborough (Roman Road) in —/07/31
c: Also known as Poison Cross Halt

d: Originally opened as Elmton
e: (R) Woodnesborough Colliery in —/07/31
f: Known as plain Canterbury Road and (R) Canterbury Road, Wingham in —/07/31

2

Gravesend and Maidstone

Contents

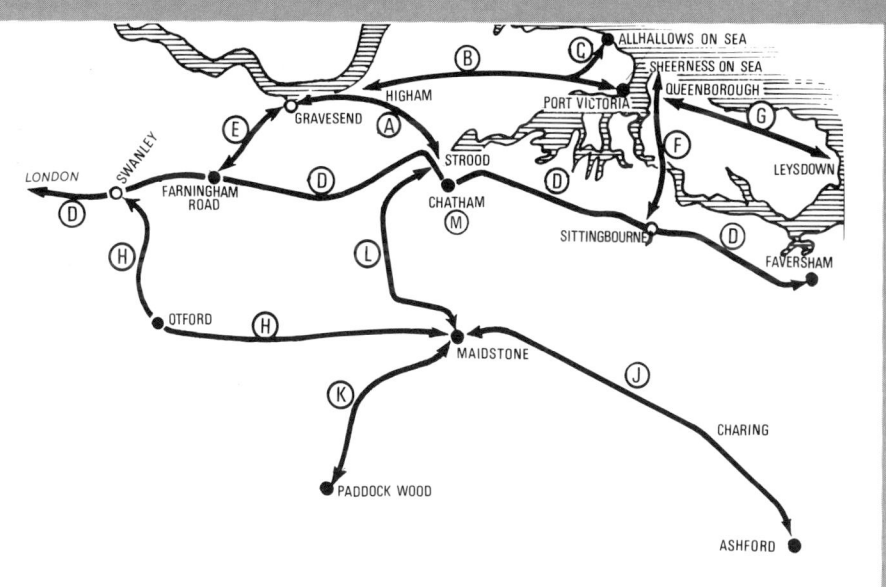

A

Gravesend & Rochester Railway

The Company
Incorporated 1845
Bought by SER 1846

Opening Dates
Gravesend (Denton)–Rochester (Strood) (original G&R line) 10/02/1845
New lines opened by SER and new Strood station

opened 23/08/1847
Through service to 2nd Strood station 30/07/1849

Closure Date
None

Line Remaining Open
Gravesend–Stood Pass/Goods

70	Gravesend (G&R)*	10/02/1845	30/07/1849	30/07/1849	30/07/1849	
71	Gravesend (SER)*®	30/07/1849	Gravesend	06/11/61	P	
72	Milton Road Halt	—/08/06	01/05/15	—	01/05/15	
73	Denton Halt*®	—/07/06	04/12/61	—	04/12/61	
74	Milton Range Halt	—/07/06	17/07/32	—	17/07/32	
75	Hoo Staff Halt*	—/—/56	(Hoo Staff Halt)	†	†	
76	Higham	—/—/1845	Higham	04/09/61	P	
77	Rochester (G&R)*	10/02/1845	13/12/1846	13/12/1846	13/12/1846	
78	Strood (1st)*	23/08/1847	18/06/1856	unaffected	see entry below	
79	Strood (SER) (2nd)*	30/07/1849	Strood	CCD 16/08/71†	P/G	

Notes to table

70 Temp. closed, 13/12/1846–23/08/1847

71 ® Gravesend Central 01/07/1899;
® Gravesend 14/06/65
G 06/11/61 except private sidings since closed

73 ® Denton Road —/11/14t;
® Denton Halt ——/10/19t

75 Unadvertised staff halt at Hoo Junction, with staggered platforms. Speedlink Sorting Sidings

77 Original Rochester station closed in 1846 and replaced by new station called Strood, when the line was doubled by the SER

78 The first station called Strood, opened when the line was doubled by the SER and replacing the original G&R station, see 77.
Station resited 18/06/1856. Strood Dock G/CC 01/11/62

79 See 78 for freight details. Private coal sidings at station

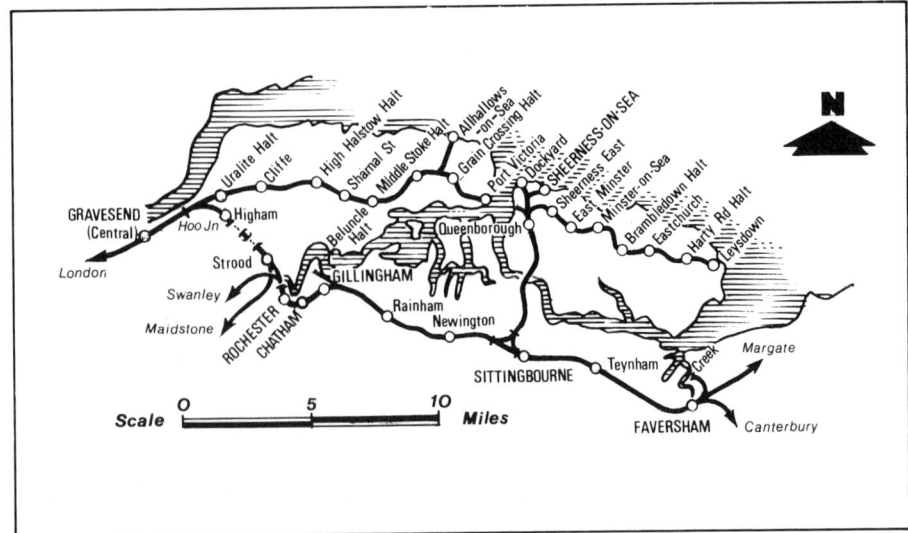

Below:
2A71   A wet day at Gravesend in December 1980 showing the now-disbanded Class 415/1 suburban unit No 5175.   *Quentin Williamson*

Bottom:
2A79   The second station at Strood opened two years after the first, in 1849, but the present location dates from 1856. Taxis wait outside the station entrance in BR days.

B

Hundred of Hoo Railway

The Company
Incorporated 1879
Absorbed into SER 11/08/1881

Opening Dates
Hoo Junction–Sharnal St 31/03/1882
Sharnal St–Port Victoria 11/09/1882

Closure Dates
Stoke Jn Halt–Port Victoria P 11/06/51

Stoke Jn Halt–Grain RO 04/09/51
(Grain Crossing Halt and Port Victoria closed from
11/06/51 and were given a replacement bus service
until the new station opened at Grain on 04/09/51)
Hoo Junction – Grain P 04/12/61

Lines Remaining Open
Hoo Jn–Port Victoria (now buried under oil refinery at
Grain) Goods only.

80	Uralite Halt	—/07/06	04/12/61	—	04/12/61
81	Cliffe*	31/03/1882	04/12/61	20/08/62†	G
82	High Halstow Halt	—/07/06	04/12/61	—	04/12/61
83	Sharnal Street*	31/3/1882	04/12/61	20/08/62†	G
84	Beluncle Halt	—/07/06	04/12/61	—	04/12/61
85	Middle Stoke Halt	—/07/06	04/12/61	—	04/12/61
86	Stoke Junction Halt	17/07/32	04/12/61	—	04/12/61
87	Grain Crossing Halt*	01/07/06	03/09/51	—	03/09/51
88	Grain*	04/09/51	04/12/61	†	G
89	Port Victoria*	11/09/1882	11/06/51	†	G

Notes to table
81 Private sidings at Cliffe serving Brett (Marine
Aggregates) Ltd terminal. G 20/8/62 except private
sidings
83 G 20/08/62 except pte sidings
87 Grain Crossing Halt closed from 11/06/51 and
served by replacement bus service until new Grain
station opened. Officially closed from 03/09/51

88 New Grain station, opened on 04/09/51 when rail
services were restored (see 87). BP's oil terminal at
Grain O 05/04/55 and swallowed up old station at
Port Victoria
89 Port Victoria closed from 11/06/51 and was served
by replacement bus service until new Grain station
opened. Station swallowed up by BP's Grain oil
terminal

C

SR, Allhallows Light Railway

The Company
Southern Railway

Opening Dates
Stoke Junction–Allhallows-on-sea
(excursion date) 14/05/32
(public opening) 16/05/32

Closure Date
Stoke Junction–Allhallows-on-sea P/G/CC 04/12/61

Lines Remaining Open
None

90	Allhallows-on-Sea*	14/05/32	04/12/61	04/12/61	04/12/61

Notes to table
90 Excursion date O 14/05/32. Public date O 16/05/32

D

East Kent Railway (Western Section)

See Line 1J for details of Eastern Section

The Company
Incorporated 1853
Ⓡ London, Chatham & Dover Railway 01/08/1859

Opening Dates
Faversham–Chatham 25/01/1858
Chatham–Rochester Bridge 29/03/1858
Rochester Bridge–Bickley 03/12/1860
Strood (SER)–Rochester (jn) (Connecting loop)
29/03/1858
Chatham Dockyard branch (goods) 16/02/1877

Closure Dates
LCDR 'Toomer Loop' closed 01/10/11 but RO 29/06/19
because of fire damage to ex-SER bridge. P/G/CC
08/01/22 when SE bridge reopened
Rochester–Strood via SER bridge TC 29/06/19ª RO
08/01/22

Lines Remaining Open
Faversham–Bickley/Strood (jn) Pass/Goods
Chatham Dockyard Goods

Remarks
a: complex junction layouts around Strood and
Rochester detailed in map

91	St Mary Cray	03/12/1860	St Mary Cray	CDO 29/01/66	P	
				07/10/68		
92	Swanley*	16/04/39	Swanley	16/05/64	P	
93	Sevenoaks Junction*Ⓡ	01/07/1862	16/04/39	16/04/39		16/04/39
94	Farningham*Ⓡ	03/12/1860	Farningham Road	20/05/68	P	
95	Fawkham*Ⓡ	—/06/1872	Longfield	07/05/62	P	
97	Meopham	06/05/1861	Meopham	02/04/62	P	
98	Sole Street	01/02/1861	Sole Street	19/04/65	P	
99	Strood*Ⓡ	03/12/1860	01/01/17	—		01/01/17
100	Rochester*	01/03/1892	Rochester	†	P/G	
101	Chatham*	25/01/1858	Chatham	†	P/G	
102	New Brompton*Ⓡ	—/—/1858	Gillingham	04/05/70†	P	
103	Rainham & Newington*Ⓡ	25/01/1858	Rainham	02/04/62	P	
104	Newington	01/08/1862	Newington	01/10/62	P	
105	Sittingbourne*Ⓡ	25/01/1858	Sittingbourne	05/07/76†	P/G	
106	Teynham	25/01/1858	Teynham	01/10/62	P	
107	Faversham*	25/01/1858	Faversham	16/08/71†	P/G	
108	Chatham Dockyard*	16/02/1877	—	†	G	

Notes to table
92 New station to replace Sevenoaks Junction. G 16/05/64 except private sidings since closed
93 Ⓡ Swanley Junction 01/01/1871. Replaced by new station at Swanley, 21 chains to the west, on 16/04/39
94 Ⓡ Farningham & Sutton 01/04/1861; Ⓡ Farningham 01/08/1861; Ⓡ Farningham Road —/09/1869†; Ⓡ Farningham Road & Sutton-at-Hone —/01/1872. Subsequently also known simply as Farningham Road for maps, timetables, etc. G 20/05/68 except private sidings later closed
95 Ⓡ Longfield 12/06/61. Full title: Longfield For Fawkham & Hartley. Longfield siding G/CC 10/08/64
99 Ⓡ Rochester Bridge 01/04/1861; Ⓡ Rochester & Strood 01/11/1861; Ⓡ Rochester Bridge (Strood) —/03/1892†; Ⓡ Rochester Bridge —/01/05†
100 Rochester & Chatham freight depot; gypsum siding; Rochester Docks

101 See 100. Chatham Dockyard (MOD) line leaves main line east of Gillingham
102 Ⓡ New Brompton (Gillingham) —/05/1886†; Ⓡ Gillingham 01/10/12; Ⓡ Gillingham (Kent) 09/07/23. Subsequently known simply as Gillingham. See 101 for details of Chatham Dockyard line. Gl Gillingham electric multiple unit depot beside station
103 Ⓡ Rainham 01/08/1862
105 Ⓡ Sittingbourne & Milton 01/07/1899; Ⓡ Sittingbourne & Milton Regis ––/05/08†; Ⓡ Sittingbourne 04/05/70. Private sidings including Bowaters china clay terminal. Continental freight yard leased to private company. G 05/07/76 except above private sidings
107 Faversham Docks freight depot. Carriage sidings
108 Chatham Dockyard (Ministry of Defence)

Above:
2D101 The LC&DR, then known as the East Kent Railway, started its life at Chatham in 1858 with the construction of the line to Faversham. This overview provides a clear picture of the station, still the main one for the Medway towns.

Below:
2D102 Class D 4-4-0 No 31577 waits at the platform at Gillingham station in a scene from the 1950s.
A. M. Pope Collection

Below:
2D102   Class C 0-6-0 No 31037 on the turntable at Gillingham shed. *A. M. Pope Collection*

Bottom:
2D104   The 1862 station at Newington, clearly showing the signalbox. The track layout at the modest country station was radically altered with electrification in 1959.

Above:
2D105 Sittingbourne in South Eastern & Chatham days, when it was known as Sittingbourne and Milton. The station opened with the line in 1858.

Left:
2D107 The LC&DR main line reached Faversham in 1858 and was extended to Canterbury two years later. Beyond the two island platforms, the lines diverged to Ramsgate and Dover.

Below left:
2D107 See previous caption.

E

Gravesend Railway

The Company
Incorporated 1881
Absorbed into the LCDR 1883

Closure Dates
Fawkham (jn)–Gravesend P 03/08/53
Southfleet–Gravesend G/CC 25/03/68
Fawkham (jn)–Southfleet G/CC date unknown

Opening Date
Fawkham (jn)–Gravesend 10/05/1886

Lines Remaining Open
None

109a	Longfield Halt	01/07/13		03/08/53	—	03/08/53
109b	Southfleet*	10/05/1886		03/08/53	11/06/62	11/06/62
110a	Rosherville Halt*	10/05/1886		16/07/33	—	16/07/33
110b	Gravesend*®	10/05/1886		03/08/53	25/03/68	25/03/68

Notes to table
109b G/CC 11/06/62 except for coal depot, since closed
110a Unstaffed from 17/06/28

110b ® Gravesend West Street 01/07/1899;
® Gravesend West 26/09/49

2E110a The unimpressive island halt at Rosherville was built in 1886, when the LC&DR opened their branch to Gravesend. It closed in 1933, twenty years before all passenger services were withdrawn from the line.

2E110b A sombre view at the end of the Gravesend branch. It opened in 1886 and the terminus became Gravesend West Street in 1899 and Gravesend West in 1949. The branch closed to passengers in 1953, but freight trains continued to run to Gravesend until 1968.

F

Sittingbourne & Sheerness Railway

The Company
Incorporated 1856
Leased by LCDR 1866

Closure Dates
Sheerness Dockyard line P 22/01/22[c]
Queenborough Pier branch P 01/03/23[a], G/CC 1939

Lines Remaining Open
Sittingbourne–Sheerness Pass/Goods
Sheerness Dockyard Goods only

Opening Dates
Sittingbourne–Sheerness (Dockyard) 19/07/1860
Sheerness (Dockyard)–Sheerness-on-sea 01/06/1883[b]
Sheerness Spur (direct line, bypassing Dockyard) 22/01/22[c]
Queenborough Pier 15/05/1876

Remarks
a: Closed 01/11/14. RO 27/12/22. Branch fell into disuse after 1933
b: Dockyard–Sheerness-on-Sea TC 08/11/14–22/01/22
c: Some sources give these dates as 02/01/22

111	Kemsley Halt*®	01/01/27	Kemsley	—		P
112a	Swale Halt*®	05/06/29	10/04/60	—		10/04/60
112b	Swale*	10/04/60	Swale	—†		P
113	Queenborough*	19/07/1860	Queenborough	16/08/71†		P/G
114	Sheerness*®	19/07/1860	22/01/22	06/05/63†		06/05/63
115	Sheerness-on-Sea*	01/06/1883	Sheerness-on-Sea	—†		P
116	Queenborough Pier*	15/05/1876	01/03/23	—/—/1939		—/—/1939

Notes to table

111 Ⓡ Kemsley. Unstaffed station

112a Kingsferry Bridge was closed on 17/12/22 for repairs for nearly a year. During that time temporary platforms were erected on either side of the river. Kingsferry Bridge North closed completely with the re-opening of the bridge on 01/11/23. The platforms to the south were officially opened as Swale Halt on 05/06/29. It was replaced in 1960 by a new station on the diverted line, following the opening of a new bridge, on 10/04/60.

112b Swale was opened in 1960 with the diversion of the line (cf 112a) and was also known as Swale for Ridham Dock, nameboards removed summer 1980. Branch line south of Swale to Bowaters paper mill and sidings for coal and steel

113 Car traffic & shipbreaking sidings, Sheerness Steel plant. G 16/08/71 except private sidings

114 ⓇSheerness Dockyard 01/06/1883. Sheerness Iron & Steel Works on spur; Medway Ports Authority sidings. Dockyard P 22/01/22 with opening of spur

115 TC (pass) 08/11/14-22/01/22. See 114 for freight

116 TC (pass) 01/11/14–27/12/22. P 01/03/23, G/CC 1939

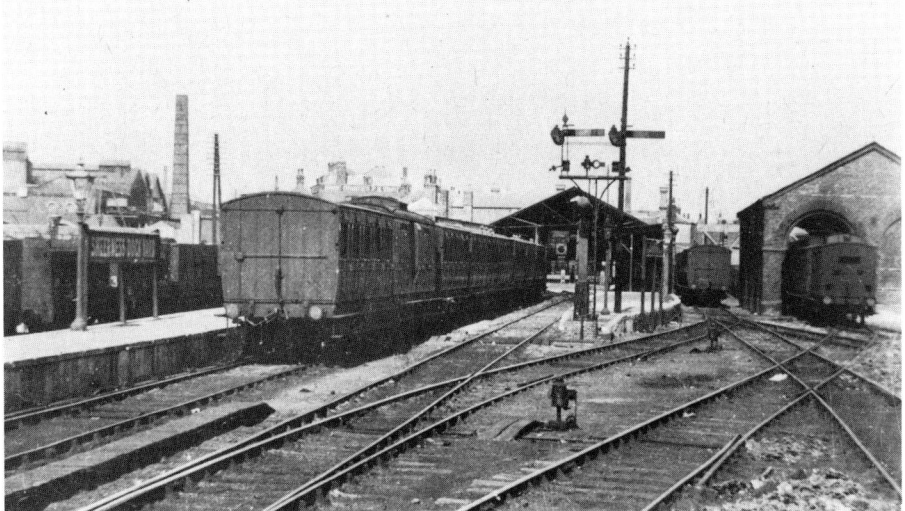

Above:
2F114 The Sittingbourne and Sheerness Railway built their line to Sheerness Dockyard station in 1860, and for more than 20 years it was a busy terminus. When the line was extended to Sheerness-on-sea, trains had to reverse at Dockyard.

Below:
2F114 A new direct line was opened in 1922 which bypassed the Sheerness Dockyard station, and passenger services were withdrawn. Freight facilities were withdrawn from the station in 1963.

2F115 Sheerness-on-sea opened in 1883 and became the new terminus for the branch. On the centre road is Class C 0-6-0 No 31584 in grubby BR livery.

G

Sheppey Light Railway

The Company
Incorporated 1899[a]
Absorbed into SE&CR 31/10/05

Closure Date
Queenborough–Leysdown P/G/CC 04/12/50

Lines Remaining Open
None

Opening Date
Queenborough–Leysdown 01/08/01

Remarks
a: Operated by SE&CR

117	Sheerness East	01/08/01	04/12/50	04/12/50	04/12/50
118	Minster (Sheppey)*®	01/08/01	04/12/50	04/12/50	04/12/50
119	East Minster-on-Sea	—/—/1902	04/12/50	—	04/12/50
120	Brambledown Halt*	—/03/05	04/12/50	—	04/12/50
121	Eastchurch	01/08/01	04/12/50	04/12/50	04/12/50
122	Harty Road Halt*	—/03/05	04/12/50	—	04/12/50
123	Leysdown	01/08/01	04/12/50	04/12/50	04/12/50

Notes to table
118 ®Minster-on-Sea 01/05/06
120 Brambledown siding G/CC 04/12/50
122 Harty Road siding G/CC 04/12/50

H

Sevenoaks Railway

The Company
Incorporated 1859
® Sevenoaks, Maidstone & Tunbridge Railway 1862[a]
Absorbed into LCDR 1879

Opening Dates
Sevenoaks Junction (Swanley)–Sevenoaks (Bat & Ball)
02/06/1862[b]
Sevenoaks (Bat & Ball)–Sevenoaks (Tub's Hill)
01/08/1869[c]
Otney (Otford, junction)–Maidstone 01/06/1874

Closure Dates
None

Lines Remaining Open
Swanley–Sevenoaks Pass/Goods
Otford–Maidstone East Pass/Goods

Remarks
a: Worked by LCDR
b: Name changes complicate opening details – please see map for clarification
c: See line 6A for details of Tub's Hill line

124	Eynsford*	01/07/1862	Eynsford	07/05/62	P	
125	Shoreham*®	02/06/1862	Shoreham (Kent)	07/05/62	P	
126	Otford*	01/08/1882	Otford	07/05/62	P	
127	Otney*	01/06/1874	01/11/1880	01/11/1880	01/11/1880	
128	Sevenoaks*®	02/06/1862	Bat and Ball	CDO 26/04/65	P	
				25/03/68†	P	
129	Kemsing	01/06/1874	Kemsing	31/10/60	P	
130	Wrotham & Borough Green*®	01/06/1874	Borough Green & Wrothan	09/09/68	P	
131	Malling*®	01/06/1874	West Malling	16/05/64	P	
132	East Malling Halt*®	—/05/13	East Malling	—	P	
133	Barming	01/06/1874	Barming	05/12/60	P	
134	Maidstone*®	01/06/1874	Maidstone East	13/09/65	P	

Notes to table
124 May have originally been spelt Eynesford. The 'ghost station' at Lullingstone was completed in 1939, between Swanley and Eynsford, but never opened
125 ® Shoreham (Kent) 09/07/23
126 Station replaced exchange platforms at the nearby junction cf 127
127 Otney comprised of exchange platforms at the junction, which were closed prior to the opening of the nearby Otford station in 1882
128 ® Sevenoaks (Bat and Ball) 01/08/1869; ® Bat and Ball 05/06/50. TC 01/01/17–01/03/19 (pass) Redland Aggregates sidings outside station
130 ® Borough Green & Wrotham 18/06/62
131 ® West Malling 23/05/49
132 ® East Malling and rebuilt in concrete 1959
134 ® Maidstone East 01/07/1899

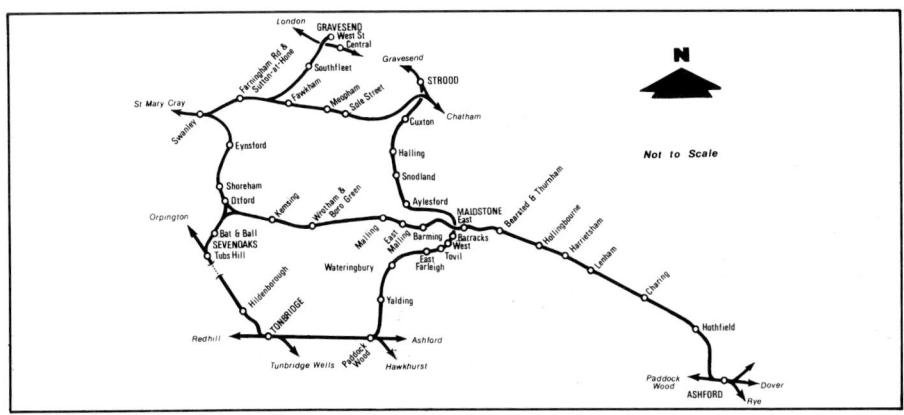

Above:
2H134 A local steam-hauled passenger train calls at Maidstone East, opened in 1874 with the line from Otford, which was absorbed in the LC&DR system in 1879.

Below:
2H134 'Battle of Britain' Class 4-6-2 No 34067 *Tangmere* climbs the 1 in 67 out of Maidstone with a down boat-train in August 1959. *Brian Coates*

J

Maidstone & Ashford Railway

The Company
Incorporated 1880
Acquired by LCDR 1881

Opening Dates
Maidstone–Ashford (LCD station) 01/07/1884[a]
Ashford (LCD)–Ashford (SER) 01/01/1892[b]

Closure Dates
None

Line Remaining Open
Maidstone–Ashford Pass/Goods

Remarks
a: running powers to SER station
b: through trains

135	Bearsted*®	01/07/1884	Bearsted	CDO 26/04/65 07/10/68	P	
136	Hollingbourne	01/07/1884	Hollingbourne	15/05/61	P	
137	Harrietsham	01/07/1884	Harrietsham	01/05/61	P	
138	Lenham*	01/07/1884	Lenham	06/01/69	P	
139	Charing	01/07/1884	Charing	16/05/64	P	
140	Hothfield*®	01/07/1884	02/11/59	22/02/64†	22/02/64	
141	Ashford*	01/07/1884	01/01/1892	†	G	

Notes to table
135 ® Bearsted & Thurnham 01/07/07, later reverted to Bearsted, —/06/80, but two signs still show Bearsted & Thurnham by request of the local council
138 G 06/01/69 except private sidings since closed
140 ® Hothfield Halt 13/08/37. Amey Roadstone

Corporation stone terminal remains open
141 LCDR station. Terminus closed to passengers with extension of line into SER station. Ashford West yard remains on site of Chatham station. Coal depot and sidings remain north of SER station

2J135 'Battle of Britain' Class 4-6-2 No 34070 *Manston* with a down boat-train outside Bearsted in September 1959. *Brian Coates*

K

SER, Paddock Wood & Maidstone branch

The Company
South Eastern Railway

Closure Dates
None

Opening Date
Maidstone Road–Maidstone 25/09/1844

Line Remaining Open
Paddock Wood–Maidstone Pass/Goods

142	Beltring & Branbridges*®	01/09/09	Beltring	05/06/61	P	
143	Yalding	25/09/1844	Yalding	27/05/63	P	
144	Wateringbury	25/09/1844	Wateringbury	04/09/61	P	
145	Teston Crossing Halt	01/09/09		02/11/59	—	02/11/59
146	East Farleigh	25/09/1844	East Farleigh	03/07/61	P	
147	Tovil*	—/—/1883/4		15/03/43	03/10/77	15/03/43
148	Maidstone*®	25/09/1844	Maidstone West	†		P/G

Notes to table

142 ® Beltring —/06/80. Transfesa international freight terminal and Rowntree Mackintosh private sidings at Paddock Wood. Beltring siding G/CC 05/06/61

147 Tovil goods depot G/CC 03/10/77

148 ® Maidstone West 01/07/1899. Station goods traffic and freight yard

Above:
2K143   The original SER station at Yalding, built in 1844, which burned down in 1893. Today a single-storey brick building stands on the Up platform

Left:
2K144   The elaborate station buildings at Wateringbury in 1886 – and again, little changed, in Southern Region days. The station opened with the line in 1844.

Above:
2K144 See previous caption.

Left:
2K146 One of the original 1844 stations on the Paddock Wood to Maidstone line, East Farleigh. BR Class H 0-4-4T No 31518 works a local passenger train on overgrown tracks.

Below left:
2K148 A rare turn-of-the-century shot at the SER's Maidstone West station. Standing at adjacent platforms are the former LC&DR engines No 476 (Kirtley Class M3 4-4-0) and No 477 (Crampton 'Tiger' Class 2-4-0). The latter engine was based at the station in its latter years, working local passenger duties until withdrawal in 1907. The numbers were allocated in 1899 with the creation of the SE&CR.

L

SER, Strood–Maidstone line

The Company
South Eastern Railway

Opening Dates
Maidstone–Strood 18/06/1856

Closure Dates
None

Lines Remaining Open
Maidstone–Strood Pass/Goods

149	Maidstone Barracks*	—/—/1874	Maidstone Barracks	—		P
150	Aylesford*	18/06/1856	Aylesford	18/04/64†		P
151	New Hythe*	09/12/29	New Hythe	—†		P
152	Snodland*	18/06/1856	Snodland	10/06/63		P
153	Halling*	01/03/1890	Halling	04/09/61†		P
154	Cuxton*	18/06/1856	Cuxton	05/06/61†		P

Notes to table
149 Opened primarily for military use
150 Allington aggregate terminal south of Aylesford

151 Reed paper terminal south of New Hythe
153 Rugby Portland cement works north of Halling.
154 Private siding remains

M

SER, Chatham branch

The Company
South Eastern Railway

Opening Dates
Strood (jn)–Rochester Common 20/07/1891
Rochester Common–Chatham Central 01/03/1892

Closure Date
Strood (jn)–Chatham Central P/G/CC 01/10/11

Lines Remaining Open
None

155	Rochester Common*	20/07/1891	01/10/11	—		01/10/11
156	Chatham Central*	01/03/1892	01/10/11	—		01/10/11

Notes to table
155 Clinker gives name of station as Rochester, ® Rochester (Central) —/12/01†
156 See map for details of route

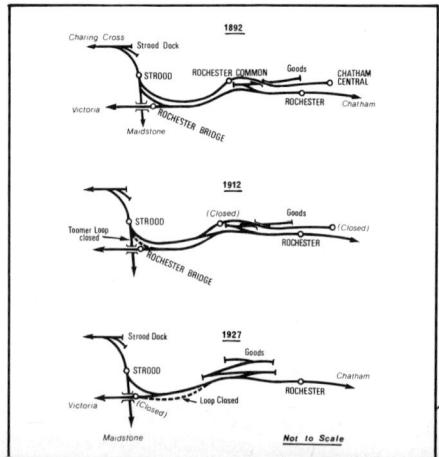

3

Tonbridge and Hastings

Contents

Appendices

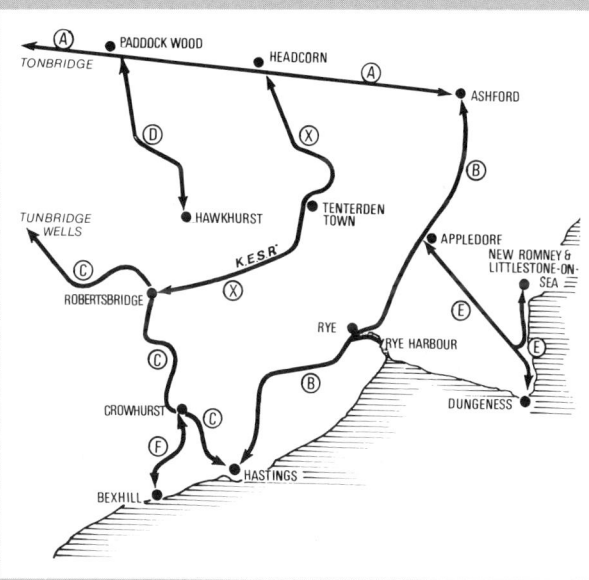

A

SER, Tonbridge line (Eastern Section) (see 6A)

The Company
South Eastern Railway

Closure Dates
None

Opening Dates
Tonbridge–Headcorn 31/08/1842
Headcorn–Ashford (private) 28/11/1842
(public) 01/12/1842

Line Remaining Open
Tonbridge-Ashford Pass/Goods

157	Maidstone Road*®	31/08/1842	Paddock Wood	03/01/66†	P/G
158	Marden	31/08/1842	Marden	03/09/62	P
159	Staplehurst	31/08/1842	Staplehurst	CCD 25/09/65	P
				04/10/71	
160	Headcorn*	31/08/1842	Headcorn	02/04/62	P
161	Pluckley	01/12/1842	Pluckley	20/09/65	P
162	Ashford*®	01/12/1842	Ashford	†	P/G

Notes to table
157 ® Paddock Wood 24/09/1844. Transfesa continental freight terminal and Rowntree Mackintosh private sidings traffic. Small marshalling yard
160 Kent & East Sussex platform P 04/01/54

162 ® Ashford (Kent) 09/07/23, later known simply as Ashford. Former SER station. Civil engineer's department sidings, crane repair shops, British Rail (AF) Chart Leacon motive power depot, carriage sidings

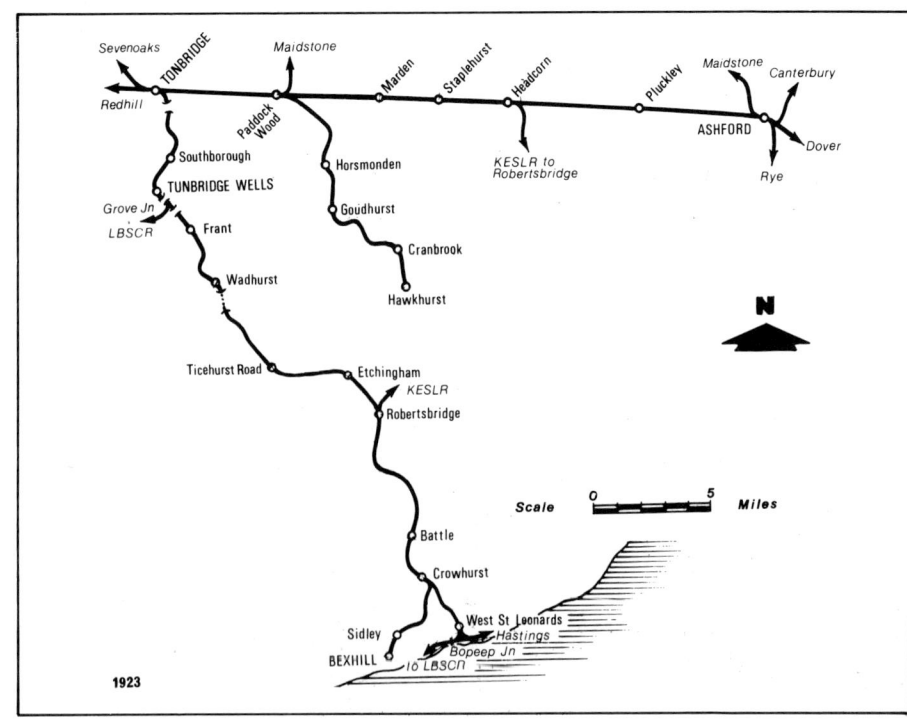

Top:
3A157   Paddock Wood was opened as Maidstone Road in 1842 and renamed two years later with the opening of the SER's first branch, to Maidstone. In 1892 it also became the junction for the Hawkhurst branch, closed in 1961. This picture shows the station in 1872.

Above:
3A160   Headcorn was opened with the original SER main line in 1842, and became a junction in 1905 with the opening of the Kent & East Sussex Railway's line from Tenterden. In this picture BR Class D 4-4-0 No 31496 passes a single-coach train at the K&ESR platform shortly before the latter line closed to passengers in 1954.

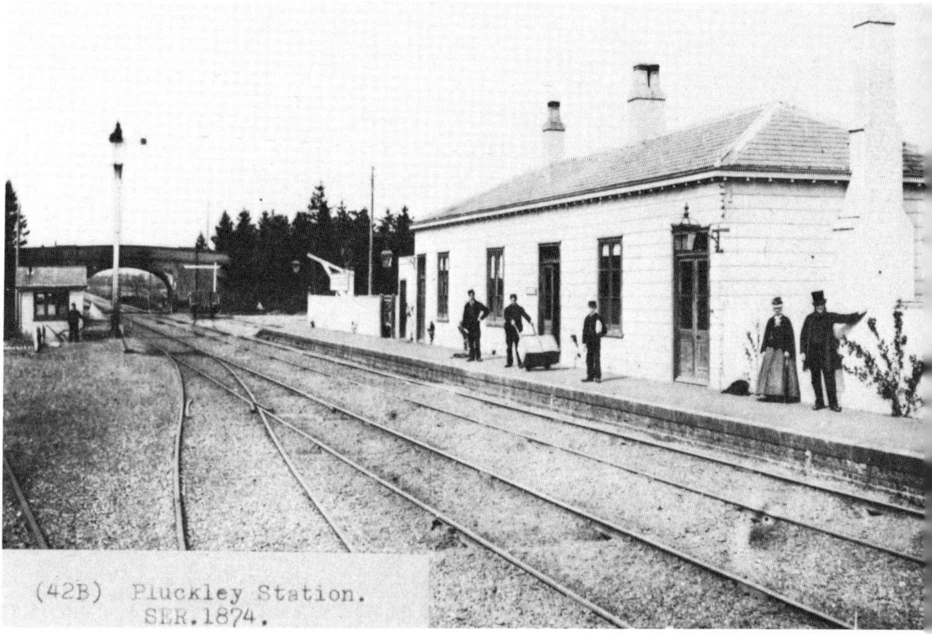
(42B) Pluckley Station.
SER.1874.

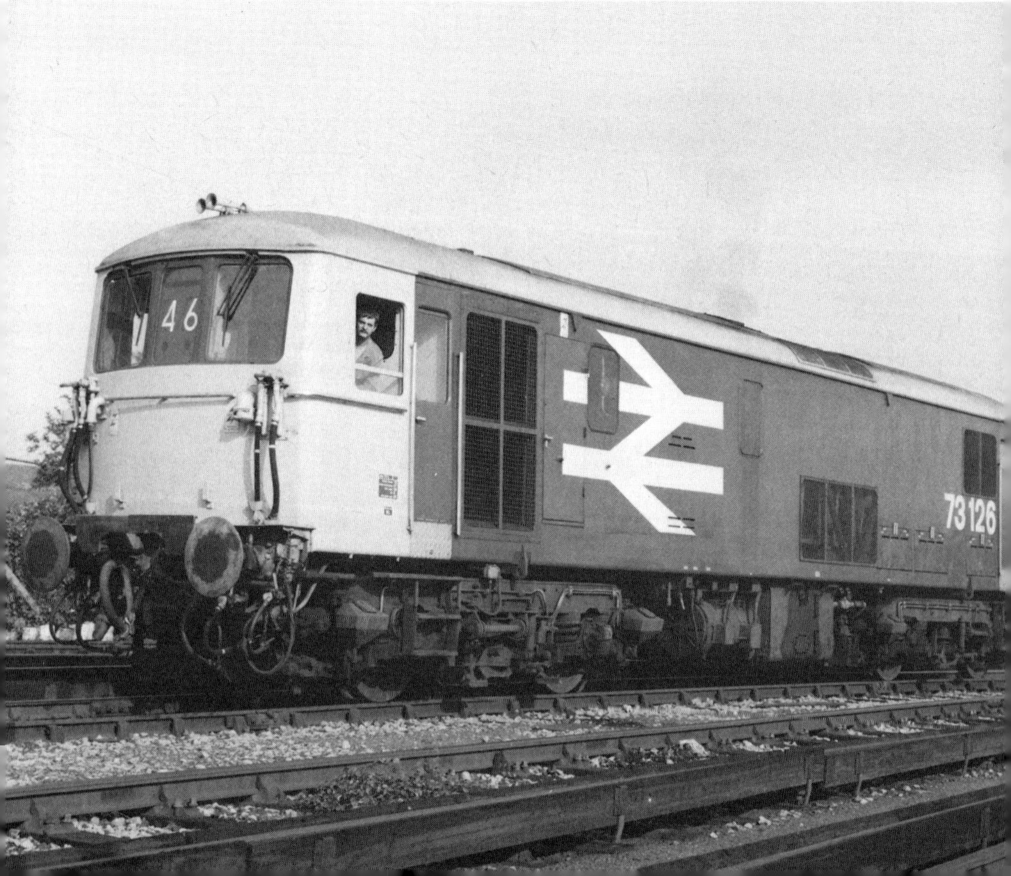
46
73126

Above left:
3A161 The distinctive wooden buildings of the 1842 station at Pluckley, outside Ashford, taken in 1874.

Left:
3A162 Electro-diesel No 73.126 stands in the Ashford loco sidings (now lifted) preparing to run light engine to Tonbridge West yard in August 1984.
Keith Dungate

Top:
3A162 Class 423 4-VEP unit No 7855 forms the front portion of an up Charing Cross train at Ashford in June, 1979. *Quentin Williamson*

Centre right:
3A162 Ashford, the hub of the South Eastern Railway, on May 12, 1891. The station opened in 1842 and the town became Kent's best-known railway centre.

Bottom right:
3A162 Class D1 4-4-0 No 31545 at Ashford shed in June, 1957. *Brain Coates*

(9B) Ashford Station.
12th May 1891.

Above:
**3A162   The old loco sidings at Ashford are the setting
as Class 47/4 diesel No 47474 waits for work in May
1984. These sidings have since been removed.**
Keith Dungate

Below:
3A162   'Schools' Class V 4-4-0 *King's Wimbledon*
**stands at Ashford shed in June 1957. The shed carried
the code 74A until 1958, and then became 73F. It
closed to steam in 1962.** *Brian Coates*

B

SER, Ashford–Hastings line

The Company
South Eastern Railway

Opening Dates
Ashford–Bopeep Junction 13/02/1851
Rye Harbour branch (goods) —/03/1854

Closure Date
Rye Harbour branch G/CC —/—/1962

Line Remaining Open
Ashford–Bopeep Junction Pass/Goods

163	Ham Street*®	13/02/1851	Ham Street	04/12/61		P
164	Appledore	13/02/1851	Appledore	27/05/63		P
165	Rye	13/02/1851	Rye	09/09/63		P
166	Winchelsea*®	13/02/1851	Winchelsea	01/05/61		P
167	Snailham Halt	01/07/07		02/02/59	—	02/02/59
168	Doleham Halt*	01/07/07	Doleham	06/02/61		P
169	Three Oaks Bridge*®	01/07/07	Three Oaks	—		P
170	Ore*	01/01/1888	Ore	CDO 23/10/65 01/05/73†		P
171	Hastings	13/02/1851	Hastings	03/05/71		P
172	St Leonards*®	13/02/1851	St Leonards (Warrior Sq)	—		P
173	Rye Harbour (Goods)	—/03/1854	—	—/—/1962		—/—/1962

Notes to table
163 ® Ham Street & Orlestone 01/02/1897, later reverted to Ham Street, early 1976
166 ® Winchelsea Halt 12/06/61 (unstaffed halt); ® Winchelsea 05/05/69
168 Doleham Siding G/CC 06/02/61. No goods at station

169 ® Three Oaks & Guestling Halt; ® Three Oaks & Guestling, ® Three Oaks late 1979
170 CEGB Power Station at Ore. Goods yard, carriage depot
172 TC 01/01/17–01/01/19. ® St Leonards (Warrior Square) 05/12/1870

3B165   A clear view of the 1851 station at Rye on the Ashford-Hastings line in June 1979 – little changed from steam days apart from the presence of Class 205

3H diesel-electric multiple-unit No 1116.
Quentin Williamson

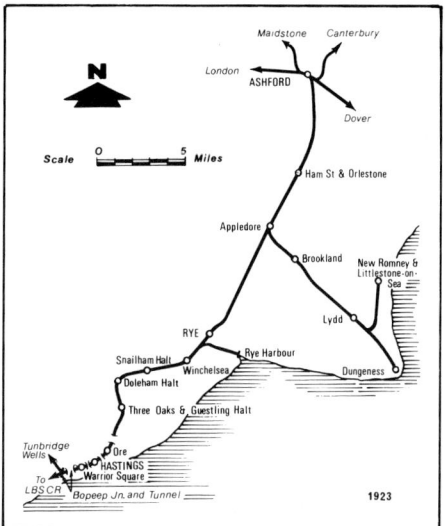

Below:
3B167 Snailham Halt was one of three unprepossessing halts on the Ashford-Hastings line opened in 1907. Whereas the others still survive as stations, Snailham closed completely in 1959.

Bottom:
3B171 The SER and LB&SCR fought a bitter wrangle over Hastings traffic when the SER opened their station in 1851. In this 1893 shot there is plenty of interesting stock on show – but the station itself was rebuilt in 1931 and freight facilities withdrawn in 1971.

Right:
3B171 Class 202 6L diesel-electric multiple-unit No 1019 at Hastings in July 1981, shortly after arriving from Charing Cross. *Quentin Williamson*

(6B)   Hastings Station. SER.

C

SER, Tonbridge–Hastings line

The Company
South Eastern Railway

Opening Dates
Tonbridge–Jackwood Springs (temp station)
  20/09/1845
Jackwood Springs–Tunbridge Wells (temp station)
  25/11/1846
Tunbridge Wells–Robertsbridge 01/09/1851

Robertsbridge–Battle 01/01/1852
Battle–Bopeep Junction 01/02/1852
Tunbridge Wells (jn, SER-LBSCR) 18/05/1881

Closure Dates
Tunbridge Wells (jn, SER-LBSCR) 06/07/85

Line Remaining Open
Tonbridge–Bopeep (jn) Pass/Goods

174	Southborough*®	—/03/1893	High Brooms	03/07/61†	P	
175	Tunbridge Wells (temp station)*	20/09/1845	25/11/1846	—		25/11/1846
176	Tunbridge Wells*®	25/11/1846	Tunbridge Wells Central	N/A	P	
177	Frant	01/09/1851	Frant	03/09/62	P	
178	Wadhurst	01/09/1851	Wadhurst	03/09 62	P	
179	Witherenden*®	01/09/1851	Stonegate	06/11/61	P	
180	Etchingham	01/09/1851	Etchingham	03/12/62	P	
181	Robertsbridge*	01/09/1851	Robertsbridge	10/06/63	P	
			06/10/69	—		06/10/69
182	Mountfield Halt*®	—/—/1923				
183	Battle*	01/01/1852	Battle	CDO 26/02/66 02/10/66†	P	
184	Crowhurst*	01/06/02	Crowhurst	05/06/61	P	
185	West St Leonards	—/—/1887	West St Leonards	—	P	

Notes to table

174 Ⓡ High Brooms 21/09/25. Oil terminal
175 Temporary station at Jackwood Springs outside Tunbridge Wells. Unlikely to have ever carried a name
176 Ⓡ Tunbridge Wells Central 09/07/23
179 Ⓡ Ticehurst Road —–/12/1851; Ⓡ Stonegate 16/06/47

181 G 10/06/63 except private sidings, since closed
182 Ⓡ Mountfield 05/05/69
183 British Gypsum Mountfield siding, north of Battle. G 02/10/66 except private sidings
184 Crowhurst siding G/CC 02/04/62

Above:
3C176 An atmospheric shot of Tunbridge Wells station in 1891. The SER station opened in 1846 and became Tunbridge Wells Central in 1923

Below:
3C181 Robertsbridge, pictured here in 1888, opened in 1851 and became the junction for the K&ESR line in 1900. Passenger trains ceased on the branch in 1954, and it closed completely in 1961.

D

Cranbrook & Paddock Wood Railway

The Company
Incorporated 1877[a]
Absorbed into SER 1900

Opening Dates
Paddock Wood–Hope Mill 01/10/1892
Hope Mill–Hawkhurst 04/09/1893

Closure Date
Paddock Wood–Hawkhurst P/G/CC 12/06/61

Lines Remaining Open
None

Remarks
a: Worked by SER. Original powers granted to build line from Paddock Wood to Cranbrook in 1877 and for extension to Hawkhurst in 1882, but never exercised. Line built under amended powers by the SER in 1887 (Cranbrook) and 1892 (Hawkhurst)

186	Horsmonden	01/10/1892	12/06/61	12/06/61	12/06/61
187	Hope Mill*®	01/10/1892	12/06/61	12/06/61	12/06/61
188	Cranbrook	04/09/1893	12/06/61	12/06/61	12/06/61
189	Hawkhurst	04/09/1893	12/06/61	12/06/61	12/06/61

Note to table
187 Full name: Hope Mill for Goudhurst and Lamberhurst; ® Goudhurst 01/12/1892

3D189   A tranquil portrait of the Hawkhurst branch terminus, opened in 1893 and closed with the line in 1961.

E

Lydd Railway

The Company
Incorporated 1881
Vested in SER 1895

Opening Dates
Appledore–Lydd 07/12/1881
Lydd–Dungeness (goods) 07/12/1881
  (pass) 01/04/1883
Lydd–New Romney 19/06/1884
Greatstone deviation 04/07/37[a]

Closure Dates
Dungeness terminus branch P 04/07/37
Appledore–New Romney (via new line) P 06/03/67
Lydd–New Romney G 18/04/64
Lydd–New Romney CC 06/03/67

Line Remaining Open
Appledore–Lydd–Dungeness (Goods only)

Remarks
a: New line 3m 65ch long, from 45ch south of New
   Romney to the Dungeness branch, 2m 10ch from
   Lydd, at Lydd Junction.

190	Brookland Halt	07/12/1881	06/03/67	—	06/03/67
191	Lydd*®	07/12/1881	06/03/67	04/10/71	04/10/71
192	Dungeness*	(g) 07/12/1881	04/07/37	—/—/1952†	—/—/1952
		(p) 01/04/1883			
193	Lydd-on-sea*®	04/07/37	06/03/67	—	06/03/67
194	Greatstone-on-sea*®	04/07/37	06/03/67	—	06/03/67
195	New Romney & Littlestone*®	19/06/1884	06/03/67	18/04/64	06/03/67

Notes to table
191 ® Lydd Town 04/07/37
192 CEGB Power station reached on freight-only
branch from Appledore
193 On Greatstone deviation. ® Lydd-on-Sea Halt and
unstaffed from 20/09/54

194 On Greatstone deviation. ® Greatstone-on-Sea
Halt and unstaffed from 14/06/54
195 ® New Romney & Littlestone-on-Sea —/10/1888†

F

SER, Crowhurst, Sidley & Bexhill Railway

The Company
Incorporated 1897[a]

Opening date
Crowhurst–Bexhill 01/06/02

Closure Dates
Crowhurst–Bexhill G 09/09/63
Crowhurst–Bexhill P/CC 15/06/64

Lines Remaining Open
None

Remarks
a: under agreement with the SER

196	Sidley*	01/06/02	15/06/64	09/09/63	15/06/64
197	Bexhill*®	01/06/02	15/06/64	09/09/63	15/06/64

Notes to table
196 Closed 01/01/17. RO for goods/coal 05/11/17; RO
(pass) 14/06/20

197 Closed 01/01/17. RO for goods/coal 05/11/17; RO
(pass) 01/03/19. ® Bexhill-on-Sea 1920; ® Bexhill
09/07/23; ® Bexhill West —/11/29

Above:
3F197   The short branch to Bexhill was only completed in 1902, after the formation of the SE&CR. The line closed completely in 1964.

Below:
3F197   Bexhill was renamed Bexhill-on-sea between 1920 and 1923, and became Bexhill West in 1929. Here BR Class H 0-4-4T No 31162 waits with one of the short branch line trains.

Appendix I:

Romney, Hythe & Dymchurch Railway

The Romney, Hythe & Dymchurch Railway is a 15in gauge private railway operating along the coastal section of the Romney Marshes and originally designed to provide an economical form of transport in that remote area.

It was the brainchild of miniature railway enthusiast Capt John Howey, and a light railway order was issued on 26/05/26. The first unofficial train ran between Jesson and New Romney later that same year, but the ceremonial opening of the Hythe–New Romney section was held on 16/07/27. The line was extended to The Pilot on 24/05/28 and, without ceremony, to Dungeness in August 1928.

The small line had a complex history, and as with many light railways, changes of name and opening and closure dates of stations tended to be poorly documented.

The line was taken over by the War Department in June 1940 and closed to ordinary traffic that month, although it was extensively used during the war. It was re-opened to the public between New Romney and Hythe during 1946 and the Dungeness section was officially re-opened on 21/03/47.

Capt Howey continued to operate the line until his death in 1963. The following year, it was purchased from his wife by two retired bankers and continued to operate much as before. In 1968 it was sold again, to a group of local businessmen, but in 1971 the new owners announced the line had no commercial future and called for a group of enthusiasts to take it over.

That group did appear, acquiring the railway on 14/02/72, and forming a holding company. The RH&DR now operates a long season from March to November, with special school trains running throughout term-time and occasional special services at Christmas.

Summary of dates
Light Railway Order issued 26/05/26
New Romney–Hythe O 16/07/27
New Romney–The Pilot O 24/05/28
The Pilot–Dungeness O August 1928
Taken over by War Department June 1940
Re-opened to the public:
  New Romney–Hythe RO 1946
  New Romney–Dungeness RO 21/03/47
Line acquired by consortium of enthusiasts 14/02/72

1	Hythe	O 16/07/27	Remains open
2	Prince of Wales Halt	O 16/07/27	Closed 1928. + May not have actually been used
3	Botolphs Bridge Halt	O 16/07/27	Disused from 1939
4	Burmarsh Road Halt	O 16/07/27	Closed to regular traffic and demolished before 1939. Also known originally as Burmarsh Rd for Dymchurch Bay & Burmarsh Village. Later Burmarsh for East Dymchurch, Dymchurch Bay and then plain Burmarsh Road. Re-opened subsequently and has handled school traffic since 1977

Below:
Hythe on 24 July 1965 with No 2 *Northern Chief* ready to leave with the 13.50 for Dungeness.
J. Scrace

5	Dymchurch	O 16/07/27	Remains open. Originally Dymchurch (Marshlands)
6	Golden Sands Halt	O Postwar	Private station. Recently closed
7	Holiday Camp Halt	O 16/07/27	Originally Holiday Camp (for St Mary's in the Marsh & Dymchurch Bay), the station was generally known as Jesson until the war, after a nearby farm. In 1946 it was renamed St Mary's Bay, and in 1981 it became Jefferstone Lane, the name it carries today
8	Warren Bridge Halt	O 16/07/27	Closed 1927. Originally known as Warren Halt. It subsequently re-opened briefly
9	New Romney	O 16/07/27	Remains open. It was known as Littlestone-on-Sea before reverting to New Romney
10	Greatstone Dunes	O 24/05/28	Closed ––/11/83 with the end of the season. Also known as Greatstone-on-Sea and as plain Greatstone. When closed, it was Greatstone Halt*
11	Littlestone Holiday Camp	O 1930s	Remains open. Opened with the camp, later known as Maddieson's Camp. Now carrying the name Romney Sands
12	Lade Halt	O 24/05/28	Closed ––/11/83 at the end of the season*
13	The Pilot	O 24/05/28	Closed ––/11/83 at the end of the season. Also known as The Pilot Inn and The Pilot Halt. It was manned until 1939*
14	Dungeness	O ––/08/28	Remains open. Originally known as Dungeness Lighthouse

*From 1981, The Pilot, Lade Halt and Greatstone Halt opened on Friday's only.

Stations Remaining Open
Hythe
Burmarsh Road (School traffic only)
Dymchurch
Jefferstone Lane
New Romney
Romney Sands
Dungeness

Appendix II:

Rother Valley Railway

The Rother Valley Railway was a rural line serving the agricultural communities of the southern Weald. It became known as the Kent & East Sussex Railway from 1904 and eventually linked two SECR main lines, the Ashford–Tonbridge and Tonbridge–Hastings routes.

Like the East Kent Light Railway, it was managed by Colonel H. F. Stephens from his office in Tonbridge – and like the Colonel's other railways, it had a distinctive atmosphere all of its own.

The southern section, from Rolvenden (originally known as Tenterden) to Robertsbridge, was opened in 1900, the stations built of corrugated iron with wooden framing. The railway was extended to Tenterden Town in 1903, but it was not until 1905 that the brick-built station appeared there: prior to the extension to Headcorn, a wooden building appears to have been used, which may then have been moved to Headcorn when the extension was opened in 1905.

The northern section featured wooden buildings similar in appearance to those on the original line, although between Headcorn and Tenterden the line was constructed to the standards of the South Eastern routes, unlike the original Rother Valley section, which had more severe weight restrictions.

The Company
Incorporated 1896
® Kent & East Sussex Railway 01/06/04
Taken over by the British Transport Commission 01/01/48 (and subsequently absorbed into British Railways, Southern Region).

Opening dates
Robertsbridge–Tenterden (Rolvenden) goods 26/03/00 pass 02/04/00
Rolvenden–Tenterden Town 16/03/03
Tenterden Town–Headcorn Junction (jn) 15/05/05

Closure Dates
Headcorn–Robersbridge P 04/01/54[a]
Headcorn–Tenterden Town G/CC 04/01/54[b]
Tenterden Town–Robertsbridge G/CC 12/06/61[c]

Re-opening dates
The Tenterden Railway Company re-opened the line from Tenterden Town to a point half-a-mile west of Rolvenden on 03/02/74. The official re-opening date was 01/06/74, by which time the line had been extended a further mile. It was further extended to

Newmill Bridge on 07/03/76 and Wittersham Road on 05/03/77. The station at Wittersham Road re-opened on 16/06/78 and the line was extended to Hexden Bridge on 25/04/83. Work is under way on a further extension to Northiam and Bodiam.

Line Remaining Open

Tenterden Town–Wittersham Road Preserved railway

Remarks

a: The Locomotive Club of Great Britain ran a special train on the line between Robertsbridge and Tenterden Town during 1958; seasonal hop-pickers trains ran to Northiam and Bodiam from Robertsbridge

b: Track lifted 1955

c: The last passenger train was an LCGB trip on 12/07/61, the last goods train the following day. Official closure was given as 12/06/61

1	Headcorn Junction (RVR)*	15/05/05	04/01/54	04/01/54	04/01/54
2	Frittenden Road	15/05/05	04/01/54	04/01/54	04/01/54
3	Biddenden	15/05/05	04/01/54	04/01/54	04/01/54
4	High Halden Road	15/05/05	04/01/54	04/01/54	04/01/54
5	Tenterden St Michaels*	—/—/1912	04/01/54	—	04/01/54
6	Tenterden Town*	16/03/03	04/01/54 RO 03/02/74	12/06/61 RO 03/02/74	Tenterden Town
7	Tenterden*®	02/04/00	04/01/54 RO 03/02/74	12/06/61 RO 03/02/74	Rolvenden
8	Wittersham Road*	02/04/00	04/01/54 RO 16/06/78	12/06/61 RO 16/06/78	Wittersham Road
9	Northiam*	02/04/00	04/01/54	12/06/61	12/06/61
10	Bodiam*	02/04/00	04/01/54	12/06/61	12/06/61
11	Junction Road Halt*	02/04/00	04/01/54	12/06/61	12/06/61
12	Salehurst Halt*	N/A	04/01/54	12/06/61	12/06/61

Notes to table

1 Known simply as Headcorn to the SECR authorities. Track lifted as far as Tenterden Town in 1955

5 Use of station provisionally sanctioned 23/04/12 and confirmed 23/11/12

6 LCGB train 1958; last passenger train LCGB train 12/07/61. Last goods, 13/07/61. Station and short section of line RO 03/02/74 by Tenterden Railway Company as a preserved steam railway. (cf notes on the re-opening of line)

7 O to goods 26/03/00 with line from Robertsbridge. ® Rolvenden 16/03/03. RO 03/02/74 (cf note 6 above)

8 RO 16/06/78 (official ceremony). cf note 6 above

9 Additional hop-pickers trains ran to station following closure. cf note 6 above. A halt was opened between Bodiam and Northiam on 23/05/81 to serve Great Dixter House. Called Dixter Halt, it was used for special railbus excursions from Bodiam, where occasional steam weekends have been held. It is not in use at present, but is available for special excursion traffic in the future

10 cf note 9 above

11 Goods sidings closed with line. Station did not feature in early timetables

12 Goods sidings closed with line except for short spur to Hodson's Mill, which was privately operated until 01/01/70. Station originally only open for goods

High Halden Road on 10 October 1953 showing K&ESR hand operated signal. *K. W. Wightman*

Reading and
Redhill

Contents

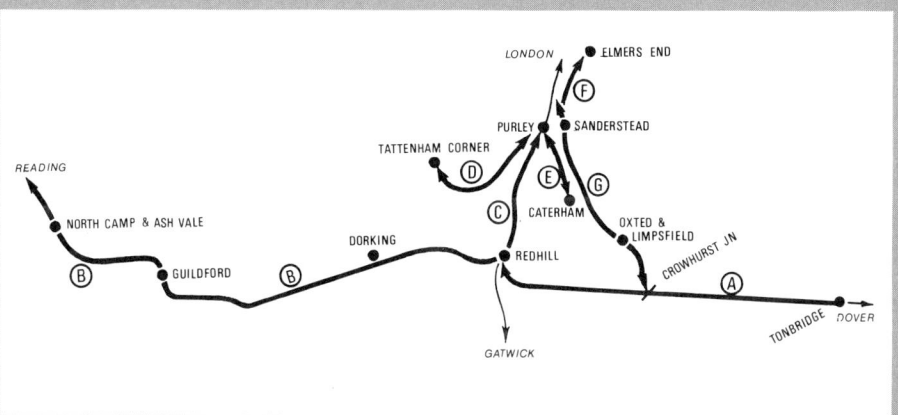

A

SER, Reigate & Tonbridge line

The Company
South Eastern Railway

Opening Dates
Tunbridge–Reigate (Redhill) (jn) 26/05/1842
(South Croydon (jn)–Crowhurst Jn (CO&EG Ry)
10/03/1884

Closure Date
Crowhurst Junction (North)–Crowhurst jn (South) P
13/06/55

Line Remaining Open
Tonbridge–Redhill (jn) Pass/Goods

198	Reigate*	26/05/1842	15/04/1844	15/04/1844	15/04/1844	
199	Nutfield	—/—/1883	Nutfield	CDO 03/01/66	P	
				G 07/11/66		
200	Godstone*	26/05/1842	Godstone	04/05/64†	P	
201	Edenbridge*	26/05/1842	Edenbridge	10/09/62	P	
202	Penshurst*	26/05/1842	Penshurst	09/09/63	P	
203	Leigh Halt*®	01/09/11	Leigh	—	P	
204	Tunbridge*®	26/05/1842	Tonbridge	†	P/G	

Notes to table
198 Old station serving Redhill and Reigate and situated east of the junction. It was closed when the new Redhill station (also originally called Reigate) was opened north of the junction. (cf. 4C 227)
200 Unstaffed from 05/11/67. Ballast tip at Godstone

201 Unstaffed from 05/11/67
202 Unstaffed from 05/11/67
203 Spelt Lyghe Halt from 1917 until c1960
204 ® Tunbridge Junction —/01/1852; ® Tonbridge Junction —/05/1893; ® Tonbridge —/07/29. Marshalling yard at Tonbridge West, freight depot at Tonbridge East. Carriage sidings

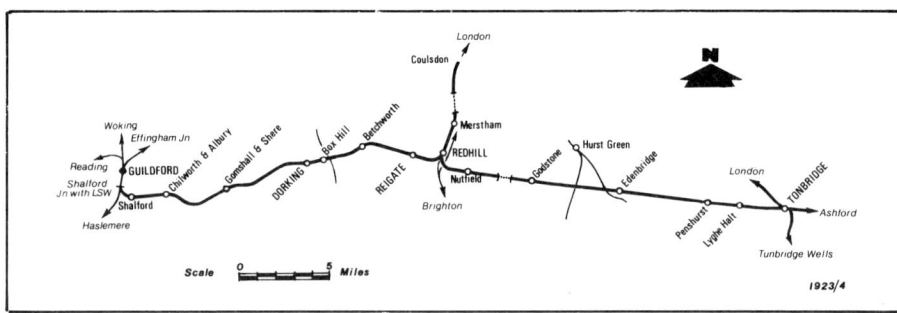

(1) Tonbridge Station. SER.
14th. Sept. 188

Below left:
4A204 Narrow-bodied Class 33/2 Bo-Bo No 33.202
leaves Tonbridge en route for Chart Leacon depot with
4-VEP No 7781 in tow on wheelskates due to severe
wheel flats, in July 1984. *Keith Dungate*

Above:
4A204 The SER's developing main line reached
Tunbridge (later named Tonbridge) in 1842. When this
picture was taken in 1888, it was known as Tunbridge
Junction.

Right:
4A204 Electro-diesel No 73.141 propels the SR
General Manager's saloon away from Tonbridge in
September 1984 after a tour by BR chairman Bob
Reid. *Keith Dungate*

B

Reading, Guildford & Reigate Railway

The Company
Incorporated 1846
Arrangements with the SER 1852

Opening dates
Reading (SER)–Farnborough 04/07/1849
Farnborough–Ash (jn) 20/08/1849
Shalford–Dorking 20/08/1849
Dorking–Reigate jn (Redhill) 04/07/1849
Reading GW/SE Junction 01/12/1858
Dorking Spur (LBSC/SE Jn) 01/05/1867
(Aldershot Jn (SE)–Aldershot Town (LSW) —/05/1879)
(Ash Jn–Guildford (LSW) 20/08/1849)
(Shalford–Guildford (LSW) 15/10/1849ª)

Closure Dates
Dorking spur not known

Lines Remaining Open
Reading–Redhill Pass/goods
Connecting lines, Reading, Wokingham, Ash, Shalford
  Pass/goods

Remarks
a: Through running began from this date

205	Reading (SER) [1st]*	04/07/1849		30/08/1855	unaffected	see entry below
206	Reading (SER) [2nd]*®	30/08/1855		06/09/65	01/10/47	06/09/65
207	Earley*	—/11/1863		Earley	06/01/69†	P
208	Sindlesham & Hurst Halt*®	01/01/10		Winnersh	—	P
209	Wokingham	04/07/1849		Wokingham	06/01/69	P
210	Wellington College*®	29/01/1859		Crowthorne	03/08/64	P
211	Sandhurst*	—/06/1852		—/12/1853t		—/12/1853t
212	Sandhurst	—/—/1923		Sandhurst	—	P
213	Blackwater*®	04/07/1849		Blackwater	CDO 06/12/65	P
					06/01/69	
214	Farnborough*®	04/07/1849		Farnborough North	14/09/59	P
215	Aldershot (North Camp)*®	—/—/1858		North Camp	06/01/69†	P
216	Ash Junction*®	20/08/1849		Ash	07/11/60	P
217	Shalford*	20/08/1849		Shalford	CDO 07/11/66	P
					G 08/05/67	
218	Chilworth & Albury*®	20/08/1849		Chilworth	07/05/62	P
219	Gomshall & Shere*®	20/08/1849		Gomshall	10/09/62	P
220	Dorking*®	04/07/1849		Dorking Town	06/05/63	P
221	Box Hill & Leatherhad Road*®	04/07/1849		Deepdene	05/11/67	P
222	Betchworth*	04/07/1849		Betchworth	28/09/64	P
223	Reigate Town*®	04/07/1849		Reigate	28/09/64	P

Notes to table
205 Closed when new SER station opened 300 yards
    further west
206 ® Reading South 26/09/49; ® Reading
    (Southern) 11/09/61. Station closed and services
    transferred to GWR station, 06/09/65
207 Shell oil terminal
208 ® Winnersh Halt 06/07/30; ® Winnersh
210 Full name Wellington College for Crowthorne,
    ® Crowthorne 17/06/28. Unstaffed from 05/11/67
211 Temporary halt
213 ® Blackwater & Sandhurst —/08/1851t;
    ® Blackwater —/06/1852t; ® Blackwater & York
    Town —/05/1897t; ® Blackwater & Camberley
    01/06/13; ® Blackwater (Hants) 09/07/23. Known
    simply as Blackwater
214 ® Farnborough North 09/07/23. Unstaffed from
    05/11/67

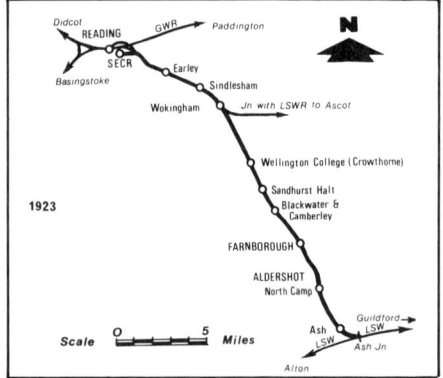

215 The station has been credited with a variety of different names, but was definitely Aldershot (North Camp) by 01/05/1879; Ⓡ Aldershot (North Camp & South Farnborough) 01/05/09; Ⓡ Aldershot (North) 09/07/23; Ⓡ North Camp & Ash Vale 30/03/24; Ⓡ North Camp 13/06/55. Oil terminal north of station

216 Ash station has also been credited with a variety of names, including Ash & Aldershot (—/07/1855), Aldershot (Ash) —/09/1858, and Ash & Aldershot again —/06/1859. By 1863 it was Ash Junction, Ⓡ Ash 01/12/26. Ash siding closed to goods on 05/12/60

217 Unstaffed from 05/11/67

218 Unstaffed from 05/11/67. Ⓡ Chilworth —/06/80

219 Unstaffed from 05/11/67. Ⓡ Gomshall —/06/80

220 Ⓡ Dorking Town 09/07/23. Carriage sidings. Unstaffed from 05/11/67

221 Ⓡ Box Hill —/03/1851t; Ⓡ Deepdene 09/07/23. TC 01/01/17–01/01/19. Unstaffed from 05/11/67

222 Unstaffed from 05/11/67

223 Ⓡ Reigate 01/11/1898. Carriage sidings outside station

Below:
4B206 The SER's long Western arm reached right into Great Western territory with the opening of Reading station in 1849. A second station opened slightly to the west in 1855 and was renamed Reading South in 1949 and Reading (Southern) in 1961. Here BR 2-6-2T No 41287 rests alongside a Southern Region EMU. The tank was Ivatt's design, introduced in 1946 on the LMS. BR continued delivery after nationalisation.

Bottom:
4B209 The substantial station at Wokingham in Southern days. It opened with the line in 1849.

4B213 The 1849 station at Blackwater became known as Blackwater & York Town around 1897 – but there were more changes of name before it reverted to its original simple name in BR days.

C

London & Brighton Railway

The Company
Incorporated 1837[a]

Opening Dates
Coulsdon (jn)–Red-hill & Reigate Road 12/07/1841
Opened to SER trains 19/07/1842
Opened to new station at Reigate (Redhill) 15/04/1844

Closure Dates
None

Line Remaining Open
Coulsdon South (jn)–Redhill Pass/Goods

Remarks
a: The L&BR had agreed to build this line and sell it on completion to the SER. Money was paid in 1843, but a dispute over the amount was not settled until —/07/1845 and the final figures agreed by the L&B board on 07/08/1845

224	Coulsdon*®	01/10/1889	Coulsdon South	01/10/31	P	
225	Merstham [1st]*	01/12/1841	01/10/1843	—		01/10/1843
226	Merstham [2nd]*	04/10/1844	Merstham	CDO 03/01/66	P	
				G 06/01/69		
227	Red-hill & Reigate Road*®	12/07/1841	15/04/1844	unaffected	unaffected	
228	Reigate*®	15/04/1844	Redhill	—/01/82†	P	

Notes to table
224 ® Coulsdon & Cane Hill —/03/1896t; ® Coulsdon East 09/07/23; ® Coulsdon South 01/08/23
225 Replaced by new station to the North. Official closure date was 01/10/1843 but the Countess of Warwick secured its re-opening until the new station was ready on 04/10/1844
226 New station north of original location. See 225
227 Redhill & Reigate Road was commonly known by

either name – ® Redhill c 1841-2t; ® Reigate —/08/1843. Replaced by new station further south
228 Replaced station further north. See 227.
® Reigate Junction 04/07/1849; ® Redhill Junction —/08/1858; ® Redhill —/07/29. Loco and carriage sidings, train holding sidings, British Industrial Sand terminal at Holmethorpe, north of station

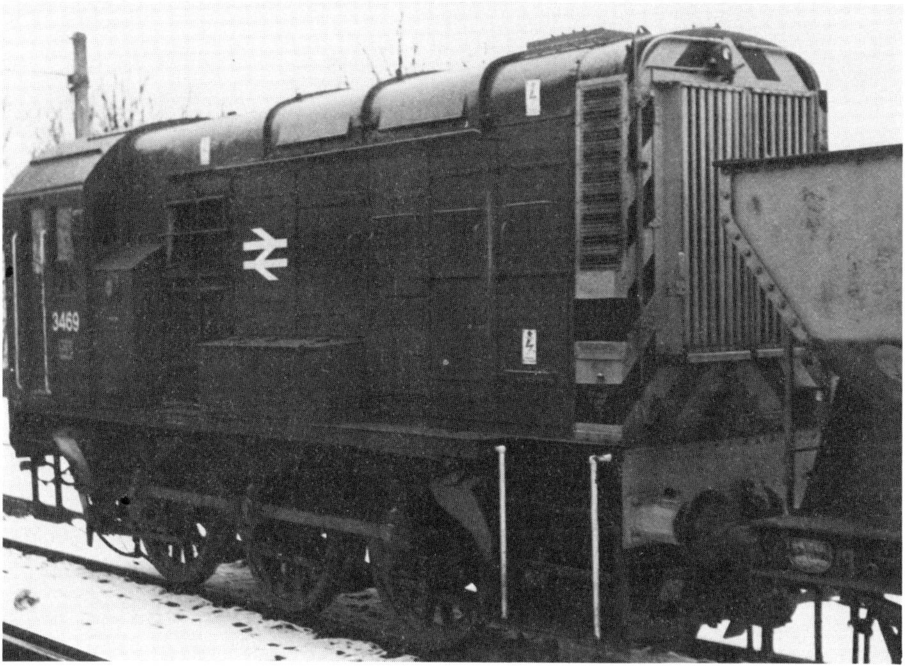

Above:
4C228 One of the ubiquitous Class 08 shunters, No 3469 (08.384) at Redhill shunting sand wagons in 1973. *Chris Sweetapple*

Below:
4C228 Class 33/2 diesel locomotive No 6589 (33.204) on a Marinex gravel train at Redhill in Spring, 1973. It was one of several Type 3 locomotives built to the Hastings line gauge. *Chris Sweetapple*

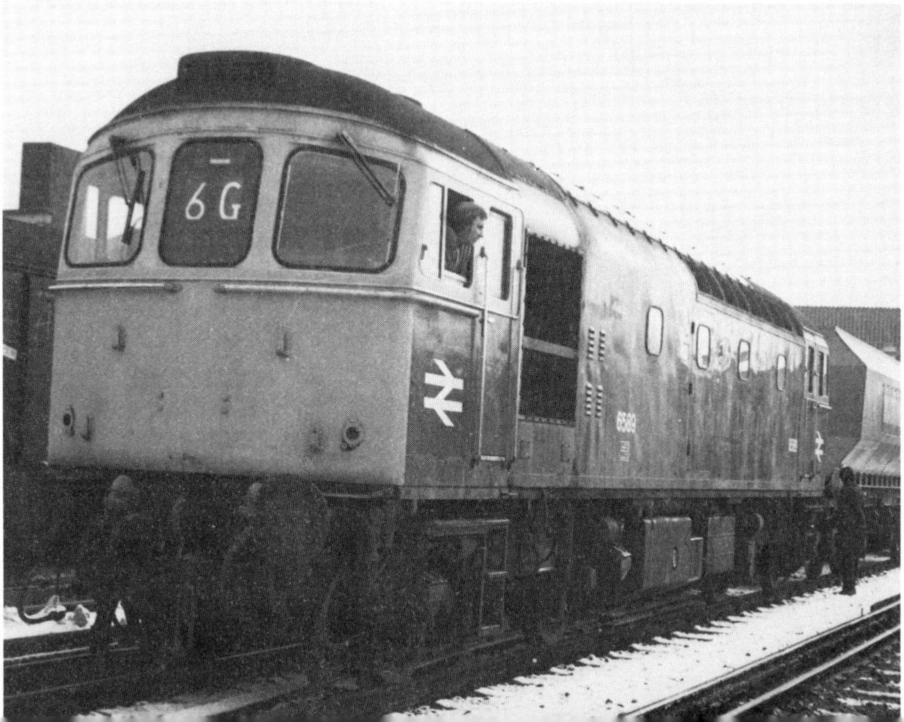

4C228 A snowy scene at Redhill, looking south, in spring 1973. The Reading line diverges to the right, Brighton straight ahead and Tonbridge to the left.
Chris Sweetapple

D

Chipstead Valley Railway

The Company
Incorporated 1893
Absorbed into SER 1899

Opening dates
Purley (jn)–Kingswood & Burgh Heath 02/11/1897[a]
Kingswood & Burgh Heath–Tadworth &
Walton-on-the-hill 01/07/00
Tadworth & Walton-on-the-hill–Tattenham Corner
04/06/01[b]

Closure Date
Purley (jn)–Tattenham Corner G 07/05/62

Line remaining open
Purley (jn)–Tattenham Corner Pass

Remarks
a: First trains 09/11/1897. Purley O 30/09/1847 as
   Godstone Road, RO Caterham Junction 05/08/1856,
   ® Purley 1888
b: Race trains only at Tattenham Corner until 1914.
   All-year-round public traffic commenced 25/03/28

74

229	Reedham Halt*®	01/03/11	Reedham	—	P
230	Smitham*	01/01/04	Smitham	07/05/62	P
231	Woodmansterne	17/07/32	Woodmansterne	—	P
232	Chipstead & Banstead Downs*®	02/11/1897	Chipstead	07/05/62	P
233	Kingswood & Burgh Heath*®	02/11/1897	Kingswood	07/05/62	P
234	Tadworth & Walton-on-the-Hill*®	01/07/00	Tadworth	07/05/62	P
235	Tattenham Corner*	04/06/01	Tattenham Corner	02/04/62	P

Notes to table

229 ® Reedham 05/07/36. TC 01/01/17-01/01/19

230 TC 01/01/17–01/01/19

232 ® Chipstead 09/07/23. First trains 09/11/1897

233 First trains 09/11/1897. ® Kingswood ––/06/80

234 ® Tadworth 01/12/68

235 Branch pick-up freight WD 07/05/62. 1901-1914 race trains only at Tattenham Corner. Station opened 25/03/28 to all-year-round public traffic

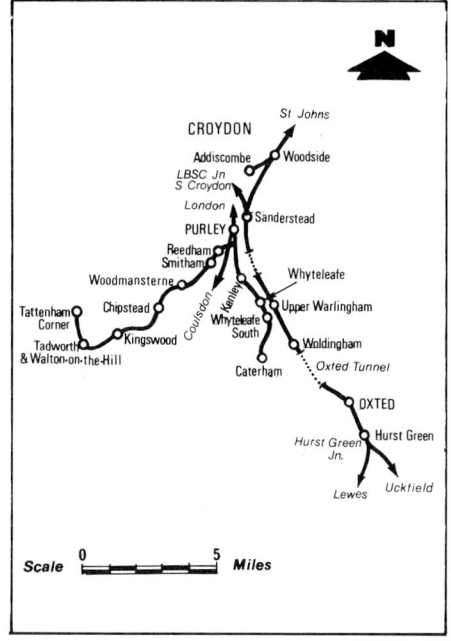

4D233 **Kingswood was the original terminus of the Chipstead Valley Railway when it opened in 1897. The impressive part-timbered buildings were set against a rural background and once included tea rooms.**

4D235 J. G. Robinson's Great Central Railway 2-8-0s became wartime standard locomotives in World War 1, serving the Railway Operating Division (ROD). Here lines of stored engines lie at Tattenham Corner, opened in 1901 to race trains and in 1928 to year-round public traffic.

E

Caterham Railway

The Company
Incorporated 1854
Bought by SER 1859

Opening Date
Caterham Jn–Caterham 05/08/1856[a]

Closure Date
Caterham Jn–Caterham G 28/09/64[b]

Lines Remaining open
Caterham Jn–Caterham Pass

Remarks
a: Purley O 30/09/1847 and RO 05/08/1856 as Caterham Junction. ® Purley 1888
b: Except private sidings since closed (Whyteleafe)

236	Coulsdon*®	05/08/1856		Kenley	03/04/61	P
237	Whyteleafe*	01/01/00		Whyteleafe	28/09/64	P
238	Warlingham*®	05/08/1856		Whyeleafe South	—	P
239	Caterham [1st]*	05/08/1856		01/01/00	unaffected	see entry below
240	Caterham [2nd]*	01/01/00		Caterham	28/09/64	P

Notes to table
236 ® Kenley —/12/1856t
237 Replaced little-used halt known as Halliloo Platform. G 28/09/64 except private sidings, since closed

238 Full name Warlingham & Cane Hill; ® Whyteleafe South 11/06/56
239 Replaced by new terminus
240 see 239

F

Woodside & South Croydon Railway

The Company
Incorporated 1880
Transferred to LBSCR/SER Joint ownership 1882[a]

Opening Date
Woodside (jn)–Selsdon Road 10/08/1885

Closure Dates
Woodside (jn)–Selsdon Road P/G/CC 01/01/17[c]
Woodside (jn)–Selsdon Road RO 30/09/35[d]
Woodside (jn)–Selsdon Road P/G/CC 13/05/83[ef]

Lines Remaining Open
None[f]

Remarks
a: Worked by SER
c: Closed as a wartime measure
d: RO to passengers with electrification of line: goods services had resumed after World War 1
e: Passenger services reduced during 1983 and withdrawn from introduction of May timetable
f: Except for oil distribution depot on spur accessible from Sanderstead direction

241	Bingham Road Halt*	01/09/06	15/03/15	—	15/03/15
242	Bingham Road*	30/09/35	13/05/83	—	13/05/83
243a	Coombe Lane*	10/08/1885	01/01/17	—	01/01/17
243b	Coombe Road*	30/09/35	13/05/83	—	13/05/83
244	Spencer Road Halt*	01/09/06	15/03/15	—	15/03/15
245	Selsdon Road*®	10/08/1885	13/05/83	07/10/68†	13/05/83†

Notes to table
241 RO 30/09/35 as Bingham Road
242 See 241
243a RO 30/09/35 as Coombe Road
243b See 243
244 Closed as a wartime measure but not reopened
245 Partially closed 01/01/17 and lay semi-derelict, although occasional Oxted line trains called. RO fully on 30/09/35 as Selsdon. Oxted line trains ceased to call from 15/06/59. Oil distribution depot remains in use north of station

4F241 Friday the 13th was unlucky for the Woodside Junction to Selsdon branch, since it was on that day in 1983 that the line closed for good. Here 2-EPB EMU No 5763 forms the 16.10 Elmers End to Sanderstead train on the last day, joining the branch at Woodside Junction. *Keith Dungate*

Below:
4F243a The original 1885 station at Coombe Lane. It closed in 1917 and was replaced by a new station called Coombe Road in 1935.

Bottom:
4F243b A modern view of the 1935 station at Coombe Road with SR 2-EPB EMU No 5763 working a local suburban service. The station and line closed for good in 1983.

Above:
4F245 When the original 1885 station at Selsdon Road re-opened in 1935 it was called Selsdon. Here Fairburn 2-6-4T No 42074 leaves with a local train in the days before electrification.

Below:
4F245 With the electrified third-rail firmly in place, Class H2 4-4-2 No 32424 *Beachy Head* brings back some nostalgic memories on an LCGB railtour.

G

Croydon, Oxted & East Grinstead Railway

The Company
Incorporated under joint ownership agreement
between LBSCR and SER 1878

Opening Dates
South Croydon (jn)–Crowhurst Jn (Oxted) 10/03/1884
(LBSCR line Crowhurst Jn–East Grinstead 10/03/1884)
(LBSCR line Hurst Green Jn–Edenbridge Town
02/01/1888)

Closure Dates
Crowhurst Junction (North)–(South) P 13/06/55[a]

Lines Remaining Open
South Croydon (jn)–Crowhurst Jn Pass/Goods

Remarks
a: Also now closed to goods

246	Sanderstead*	10/03/1884	Sanderstead	20/03/61	P
247	Riddlesdown	05/06/27	Riddlesdown	—	P
248	Upper Warlingham*®	10/03/1884	Upper Warlingham	04/05/64	P
249	Marden Park*®	01/07/1885	Woldingham	04/05/59	P
250	Oxted & Limpsfield*®	10/03/1884	Oxted	06/01/69	P
251	Hurst Green Halt*®	01/06/07	Hurst Green	—	P

Notes to table
246 See 4F 245 for notes on Selsdon, where Oxted
line trains ceased to call on 15/06/69
248 ® Upper Warlingham & Whyteleafe 01/01/1894;
® Upper Warlingham 01/10/00

249 ® Woldingham 01/01/1894
250 ® Oxted
251 ® Hurst Green 12/06/61. New station about 10ch
north of former halt

4G248   Upper Warlingham station on 7 June 1967.
J. Scrace

5

London and North Kent

Contents

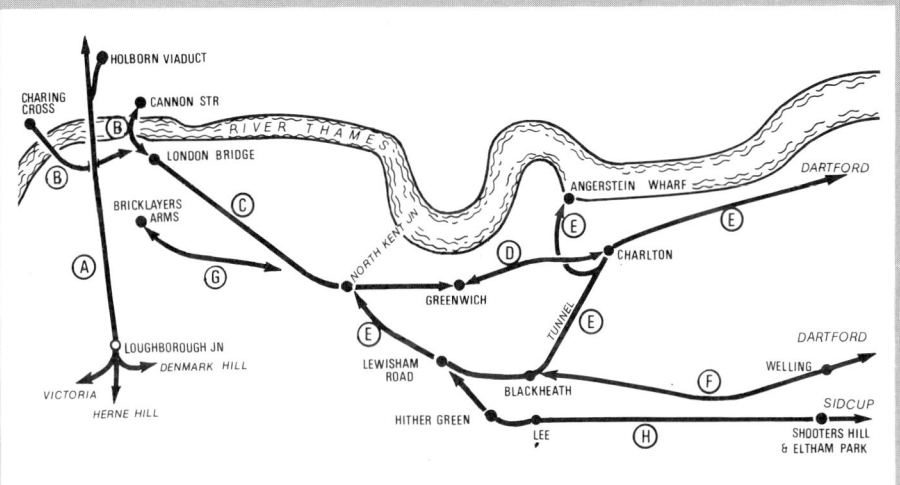

A

LCDR, City line and links

The Company
London, Chatham & Dover Railway[a]

Opening Dates
Herne Hill (jn)–Elephant & Castle 06/10/1862
Brixton (jn)–Loughborough Rd (jn) 01/05/1863
Elephant & Castle–Blackfriars Bridge 01/06/1864
Blackfriars Bridge–Ludgate Hill (temp station)
 21/12/1864
Ludgate Hill (perm station) 01/06/1865
Brixton (Canterbury Rd Jn)–LBSCR Jn–Cow Lane Jn
 01/08/1865
Ludgate Hill (Earl St Jn)–Farringdon Street (West Street
 Jn) 01/01/1866
LCDR/LBSCR Jn, East Brixton 01/05/1867
Snow Hill–Aldersgate (LCD/Met Jn, The Smithfield
 Curve) 01/09/1871
Cambria Road Junction spur (east side of
 Loughborough Rd) 01/07/1872
Holborn Viaduct terminus line 02/03/1874
Blackfriars (jn)–Metropolitan Jn (SER) 01/06/1878
Blackfriars–Ludgate Hill (via St Pauls) 10/05/1886

Closure Dates
Holborn Low Level–Farringdon Street (local services) P
 01/07/08
Holborn Low Level–Farringdon Street (through trains)
 P 11/01/15
Holborn Low Level–Aldersgate Street P/G/CC 02/04/16
Blackfriars Bridge–West St Jn G 24/03/69[b]
Blackfriars Bridge–West St Jn CC 03/05/71
Holborn Low Level–Ludgate Hill (jn) P 01/06/16
Blackfriars (jn)–Metropolitan Jn (through trains to
 GNR) P 01/05/07
Brixton (jn)–Loughborough Junction P 03/04/16

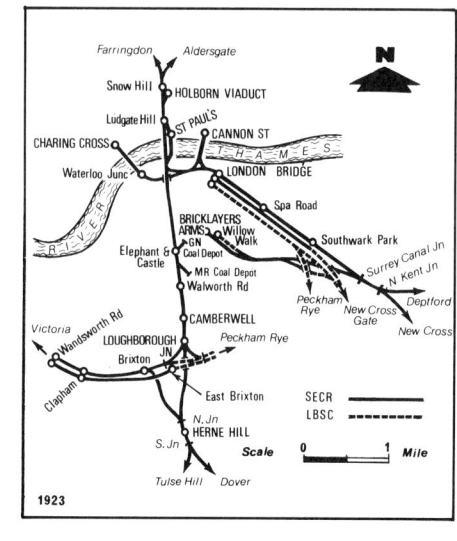

1923

Lines Remaining open
Holborn Viaduct–Herne Hill Pass/Goods
Blackfriars (jn)–Metropolitan Junction Goods
Brixton (jn)–Loughborough Junction Goods
Cambria Rd jn spur and South London line Pass/Goods

Notes:
a: See introduction for details
b: Last scheduled goods train 23/03/69

252	Loughborough Road*®	—/—/1864	Loughborough Junction	—	P
253	Camberwell*®	06/10/1862	03/04/16	18/04/64	18/04/64
254	Camberwell Gate*®	01/05/1863	03/04/16	—	03/04/16
255	Elephant & Castle*	06/10/1862	Elephant & Castle	—	P
256	Borough Road	01/06/1864	01/04/07	—	01/04/07
257	Blackfriars Bridge*®	01/06/1864	01/10/1885	unaffected	see entry below
258	Blackfriars Bridge*®	N/A	—	03/02/64	03/02/64
259	Ludgate Hill (temp)*	21/12/1864	01/06/1865	—	01/06/1865
260	Ludgate Hill (perm)*	01/06/1865	03/03/29	—	03/03/29
261	Snow Hill*®	01/08/1874	01/06/16	—	01/06/16
262	St Pauls*®	10/05/1886	Blackfriars	—†	P
263	Holborn Viaduct*®	02/03/1874	Holborn Viaduct	—†	P

Notes to table
252 Brixton spur platforms O 1864; main line and
 Cambria Rd Spur platforms O 01/12/1872 and
 station ® Loughborough Junction. Brixton spur

platforms P 03/04/16; Cambria Rd spur platforms
 P 12/07/25
253 ® Camberwell New Road 01/05/1863;
 ® Camberwell 01/10/08

254 ® Walworth Road 01/01/1865. Former coal sidings and MR coal depot north of station. MR Coal depot O 1871, transferred to S. Region 01/05/50, closed 1958 RO 21/09/59

255 Resited to permanent station —/02/1863. GN coal depot north of station O 1871 G/CC 01/07/63

257 The original terminus at Blackfriars lasted little more than six months before the route moved on to Ludgate Hill and Blackfriars Bridge became part of the goods depot. It was renamed Blackfriars between 1900 and 1904 and continued to carry freight until services were run down during the 1960s. The last official goods train, a parcels train, ran on 23/03/69, and thereaftrer there was only sporadic use before the old bridge closed completely on 03/05/71

258 See 257

259 Temporary station, replaced by new buildings 01/06/1865

260 See 259

261 ® Holborn Viaduct (Low Level) 01/05/12

262 ® Blackfriars 01/02/37 with opening of the St Pauls underground station (LT). Carriage sidings

263 ® Holborn Viaduct (High Level) 01/05/12; later reverted to plain Holborn Viaduct. Carriage sidings

B

Charing Cross Railway

The Company
Incorporated 1859
Absorbed into SER 1864

Opening Dates
London Bridge–Charing Cross 11/01/1864
Waterloo Junction–Waterloo (LSWR) 11/01/1864
Hampstead Rd Jn–Cannon Street (and loops) 01/09/1866

Closure Dates
Waterloo Junction–Waterloo (LSWR) Regular services w/d 01/01/1868[a], P/G/CC —/03/11

Storey Street. Jn–Metropolitan Junction (west loop) P 10/07/67

Lines Remaining Open
London Bridge–Cannon Street/Charing Cross Pass/Goods
Cannon St (Storey Street Jn)–Metropolitan Jn Goods

Remarks
a: Stock movements and royal trains continued

264	Blackfriars*	11/01/1864	01/01/1869	—		01/01/1869
265	Waterloo Junction*®	01/01/1869	Waterloo East	—		P
266	Charing Cross*	11/01/1864	Charing Cross	—		P
267	Cannon Street*	01/09/1886	Cannon Street	—		P

Notes to tables
264 SER station: originally planned to be called Great Surrey Street, it was also unofficially known as Blackfriars Road.

265 ® Waterloo 07/07/35; ® Waterloo East 02/05/77

266 Temp closed 05/12/05–19/03/06 after roof collapse

267 Temp closed 05/06/26–28/06/26 for suburban electrification; temp closed 02/08/74-09/09/74 for remodelling and resignalling

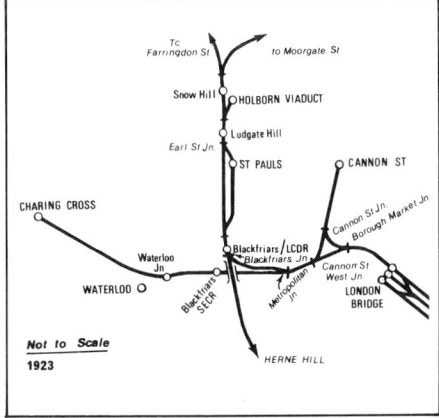

CHARING CROSS
To Farringdon St
to Moorgate St
Snow Hill
HOLBORN VIADUCT
Earl St Jn.
Ludgate Hill
ST PAULS
CANNON ST
Waterloo Jn
Blackfriars/LCDR
Blackfriars Jn
Cannon St Jn.
Borough Market Jn
WATERLOO
Blackfriars SECR
Metropolitan Jn
Cannon St West Jn
LONDON BRIDGE
Not to Scale
1923
HERNE HILL

**5B266   Refurbished class 411 4-CEP EMUs Nos 1540
and 1528 wait at Charing Cross with the 14.25
Ramsgate service in March, 1985.**   *Keith Dungate*

C

London & Greenwich Railway

The Company
Incorporated 1833
Leased to SER 01/01/1845
Company dissolved 03/01/23

Opening Dates
Spa Road (temp station)–Deptford 08/02/1836
Spa Road (temp station)–London Bridge 14/12/1836
(official)[a]
Deptford–Greenwich (temp station) 24/12/1838
Greenwich (temp station)–(perm station) 12/04/1840

Closure Dates
None

Line Remaining Open
London Bridge–Greenwich Pass/Goods

Remarks
a: Actual date, 01/12/1836. 14/12/1836 was date of
   official London Bridge–Deptford opening
   London Bridge–Corbetts Lane Jn (L&G) 01/12/1836
   Opened to London & Croydon Ry trains 05/06/1839
   Opened to London & Brighton Ry trains 12/07/1841
   Opened to South Eastern Ry trains 26/05/1842
   Through lines 11/01/1864

268	London Bridge (L&G)*	14/12/1836	see entry 271 below		
269	London Bridge (L&C)*	05/06/1839	see entry 271 below		
270	London Bridge (Joint)*	—/07/1844	see entry 271 below		
271	London Bridge (SER new)*	03/01/1851	London Bridge	N/A	P
272	London Bridge (LBSCR new)*	03/01/1851	London Bridge	N/A	P
273	Spa Road (temp)*	08/02/1836	14/12/1836	—	14/12/1836
274	Spa Road (perm)*®	30/10/1842	15/03/15	—	15/03/15
275	Southwark Park*	01/10/02	15/03/15	03/10/60	03/10/60
276	Commercial Docks	—/07/1856	31/12/1866	—	31/12/1866
277	Deptford (L&G)*	08/02/1836	24/12/1838	—	24/12/1838
278	Deptford [2nd]*	24/12/1838	15/03/15	15/03/15	15/03/15
279	Deptford [3rd]	19/07/26	Deptford	—	P
280	Greenwich (temp)	24/12/1838	12/04/1840	unaffected	see entry below
281	Greenwich [2nd]*	12/04/1840	11/01/1877	unaffected	see entry below
282	Greenwich [3rd]	11/01/1877	Greenwich	—	P

Notes to table

268 Original London & Greenwich terminus, known as the "low level" and demolished in the 1976 station reconstruction

269 Original London & Croydon terminus. L&BR and SER trains were allowed access to both stations at London Bridge over L&G and L&C lines. In a re-organisation in 1844 the owning companies exchanged their stations and extended both. A site used by the L&C to house L&BR freight services came into the ownership of the L&GR but was still used for L&B goods trains. The new station was opened incomplete in —/07/1844. No freight was carried by the L&GR

270 In —/08/1849 the L&BR goods depot was taken over by the SER as a passenger station for Greenwich line trains and the LBSCR took over the goods warehouse and empty carriage shed on the south side of the Joint station. The joint station was dissolved on 01/08/1850; the Greenwich viaduct was widened and SER station enlarged from 24/02/1850

271 From 03/01/1851 the SER and LBSCR had separate stations at London Bridge, which were only amalgamated with grouping in 1923 when both became part of the Southern Railway. The SER main line terminus of 1851, known as London Bridge Low Level, was used for continental freight between 1864 and 1901

272 See 271

273 The temporary station was closed in 1838 according to Bradshaw

274 See 273. Alternative sources give an opening date of —/09/1842. Station resited again in 1867. Full name Spa Road & Bermondsey, ® Spa Road (Bermondsey) —/10/1877.

275 A goods depot called Southwark opened in 1901 for continental freight. Closed to goods 1960 except parcels traffic, since closed.

277 Temporary station. L&G engine shed at Deptford closed —/11/04

278 TC 15/03/15-19/07/26

281 Resited 1877

5C271 London Bridge station had a long and complex history, dating from 1836. It was only after the Grouping in 1923 that the separate stations were finally amalgamated. It is seen here on a grey day in 1926 with the Southern Railway firmly in control.

D

SER, Woolwich line

The Company
South Eastern Railway[a]

Opening Dates
Charlton–Maze Hill 01/01/1873
Maze Hill–Greenwich 01/02/1878

Closure Dates
None

Line remaining Open
Greenwich–Charlton Pass/Goods

Remarks
a: See introduction

283	Greenwich (Maze Hill)*®	01/01/1873	Maze Hill	—	P
284	Coombe Farm Lane*®	—/—/1879	Westcombe Park	—	P

Notes to table
283 ® Maze Hill & East Greenwich 01/02/1878; ® Maze Hill & Greenwich Park 01/07/1878; ® Maze Hill (East Greenwich) 01/01/1899; ® Maze Hill (East Greenwich) for National Maritime Museum 02/05/37; ® Maze Hill for National Maritime Museum 04/07/37. On maps and time-tables simply Maze Hill

284 ® Westcombe Park

E

SER, North Kent Railway

The Company
South Eastern Railway[a]

Opening Dates
North Kent East Jn–Denton (Gravesend) via Charlton 30/07/1849
Angerstein Wharf branch Goods only —/10/1852

Closure Date
Angerstein Wharf branch 29/07/56 (except pte sidings)

Lines Remaining Open
North Kent East Jn–Gravesend Pass/Goods
Angerstein Wharf branch Pte sidings

Remarks
a: See introduction. Wharf branch opened by John Angerstein and leased by SER from 1892

285	North Kent Junction*	N/A	01/10/1850	—		01/10/1850
286	New Cross*®	—/10/1850	New Cross	—	P	
287	St Johns	01/06/1873	St. Johns	—	P	
288	Lewisham*®	30/07/1849	Lewisham	06/05/63	P	
289	Blackheath	30/07/1849	Blackheath	06/05/63	P	
290	Charlton*	30/07/1849	Charlton	—†	P	
291	Woolwich Dockyard	30/07/1849	Woolwich Dockyard	—	P	
292	Woolwich Arsenal*	01/11/1849	Woolwich Arsenal	G17/05/65 CCD 04/12/67†	P	
293	Plumstead*	16/07/1859	Plumstead	G 17/05/65 CCD 04/12/67†	P	
294	Church Manor Way Halt	01/01/17	01/01/20			01/01/20
295	Abbey Wood	1850	Abbey Wood	05/12/60	P	
296	Belvedere*	—/03/1859	Belvedere	10/06/63†	P	
297	Erith	30/07/1849	Erith	07/10/68	P	

298	Slades Green*®	01/07/00	Slade Green	—†	P
299	Dartford	30/07/1849	Dartford	01/05/72	P
300	Stone Crossing Halt*®	02/11/08	Stone Crossing	—	P
301	Greenhithe*	30/07/1849	Greenhithe	—	P
302	Swanscombe Halt*®	02/11/08	Swanscombe	—†	P
303	Northfleet*	1849	Northfleet	CDO 26/04/65 09/09/68†	P

Notes to Table

285 SER exchange platforms

286 Originally New Cross & Naval School. Later plain New Cross

288 ® Lewisham Junction 1857; ® Lewisham 07/07/29

290 Wharf line remains open: Thames Metal private sidings, Marcon aggregate terminal. Charlton sidings G/CC 20/05/63

292 Plumstead and Woolwich Arsenal goods amalgamated 01/11/50 as Plumstead. G 17/05/65; closed 04/12/67 except freight depot and coal depot. Paper terminal opened 08/12/71, closed 28/02/72. Carriage sidings

293 See 292

296 Goods closed except British Gypsum siding at Crabtree, out of use for several years

298 ® Slade Green 21/09/53. BR's electric multiple-unit depot, code SG

300 ® Stone Crossing

301 Ingress Abbey Platform on short branch east of Greenhithe was open during World War 1 from c1915-1919, serving a military hospital

302 ® Swanscombe. Blue Circle group has a standard-gauge system at Swanscombe cement works. Swanscombe station resited 06/07/30

303 Blue Circle Cement Works at Northfleet, BR service inaugurated 17/07/70. cf line 2A for G&R stations at Gravesend

5E288   Class 415/1 4-EPB suburban electric multiple-unit No 5194 calls at Lewisham on its way from Charing Cross to Dartford via Bexleyheath in December, 1980. *Quentin Williamson*

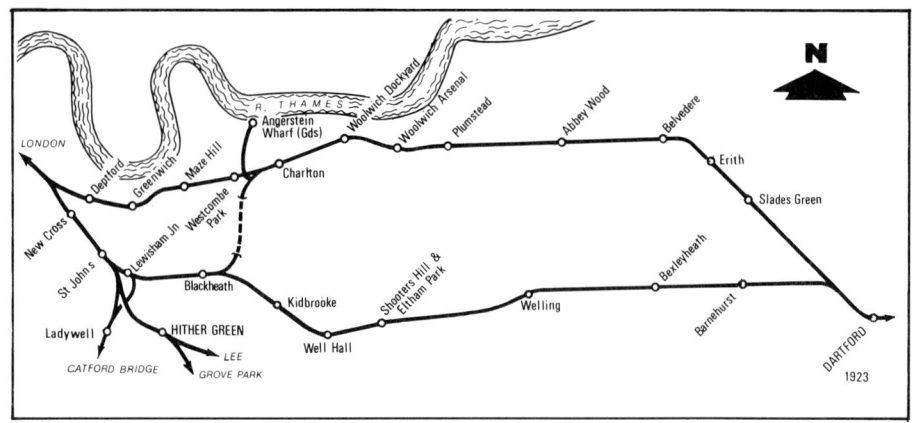

F

Bexley Heath Railway

The Company
Incorporated 1887[a]
Absorbed by the SER 1900

Opening Date
Blackheath (jn)–Dartford (jn) via Bexleyheath
01/05/1895

Closure Dates
None

Line Remaining Open
Blackheath (jn)–Dartford (jn) Pass/Goods

Remarks
a: Worked by the SER. Original line authorised in 1883, running from a junction with the Dartford loop line near Hither Green. Amended powers 1887

305	Kidbrooke	01/05/1895	Kidbrooke	CDO 26/04/65 07/10/68	P	
306a	Well Hall*®	01/05/1895	18/03/85	CDO 28/12/64 07/10/68	18/03/85	
306b	Eltham*	17/03/85	Eltham	—	P	
307	Shooters Hill & Eltham Park*®	01/07/08	18/03/85	—	18/03/85	
308	Falconwood	01/01/36	Falconwood	—	P	
309	Welling	01/05/1895	Welling	03/12/62	P	
310	Bexley Heath*®	01/05/1895	Bexleyheath	CDO 28/12/64 07/10/68	P	
311	Barnehurst	01/05/1895	Barnehurst	CDO 30/11/64 07/10/68	P	

Notes to table
306a ® Well Hall & North Eltham 01/10/16; ® Eltham Well Hall 01/10/27. Replaced by new station, Eltham, located between Eltham Park and Eltham Well Hall. Original closure date 02/03/85, but delayed because of bad weather. Last train ran early on Sunday morning, 17/03/85
306b New station, replacing Park and Well Hall
307 ® Eltham Park 01/10/27. Originally due to close

02/03/85 but delayed because of bad weather. Last train ran early on Sunday morning, 17/03/85
310 ® Bexleyheath

5F306a Eltham Well Hall on 12 September 1968. This station and the nearby Eltham Park were replaced by a new station opened in 1985. *J. Scrace*

G

SER, Bricklayers Arms branch

The Company
The London & Croydon Railway and South Eastern Railway were keen to establish a new terminus as close to London Bridge as possible. The line was two-thirds owned by the SER and one-third by the L&CR, costs being met in the same proportions. The L&CR was bought out in 1845 by the SER.

Opening Dates
Bricklayers Arms Jn (LBSCR)–Bricklayers Arms 01/05/1844
North Kent West Jn–Surrey Canal Jn 01/09/1849

Closure Dates
Bricklayers Arms branch P —/01/1852[a], G 01/08/77[b], CC 01/07/81[c], Line disused from Spring 1984

Remarks
a: Some troop trains used station 1914-1918 and some summer excursion trains 1932-1939
b: Coal and parcels traffic continued
c: Official date. Last train 20/06/81. Trains ran to crane repair depot until early 1984

312 Bricklayers Arms*	01/05/1844	—/01/1852	01/08/77	01/07/81

Notes to table
312 SER locomotive depot O 1845, closed June, 1962. Diesel maintenance depot until 1969. BR shedcode: 73B.
Willow Walk (LBSCR goods depot) O —/07/1849. Bricklayers Arms and Willow Walk goods depots merged 07/03/32. Coal depot, parcels depot O 05/05/69. Run as freight-only branch until 01/08/77, after which coal and parcels traffic continued. After complete closure of the depot in 1981, the branch was operated as a siding to the crane repair depot until these facilities were transferred to Ashford in 1984

H

SER, Dartford loop

The Company
South Eastern Railway

Closure Dates
None

Opening Dates
Hither Green–Dartford 01/09/1866
Crayford Curve (gds) 11/10/42

Lines Remaining Open
Hither Green–Dartford Pass/goods
Crayford curve Goods

313	Lee*	01/09/1866	Lee	CDO 30/11/64		P
				07/10/68		
314	Eltham*®	01/09/1866	Mottingham	CDO 13/11/65		P
				07/10/68		
315	Pope Street*®	01/04/1878	New Eltham	13/05/63		P
316	Sidcup	01/09/1866	Sidcup	CDO 30/11/64		P
				15/08/66		
317	Albany Park	07/07/35	Albany Park	—		P
318	Bexley	01/09/1866	Bexley	07/05/63		P
319	Crayford*	01/09/1866	Crayford	04/01/65†		P

Notes to table
313 Full name Lee for Burnt Ash
314 ® Eltham & Mottingham 01/01/1892; ® Eltham for Mottingham ––/04/16; ® Eltham & Mottingham ––/10/22; ® Mottingham 01/10/27

315 ® New Eltham & Pope Street 01/01/1886; ® New Eltham 01/10/27
319 Loop to Slade Green used for occasional passenger trains and empty coaching stock

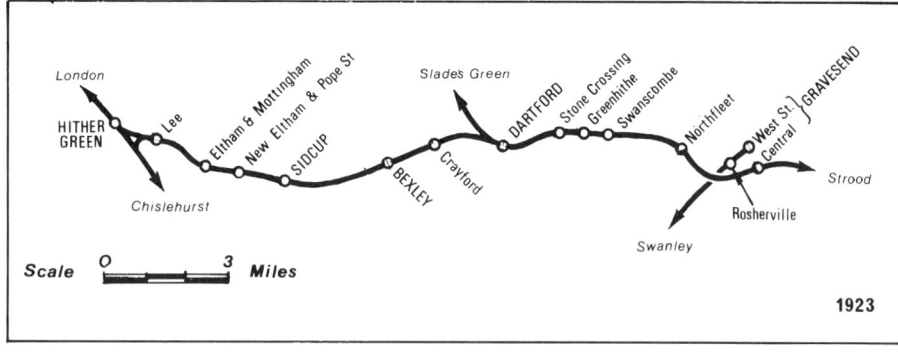

1923

6

Southeast London

Contents

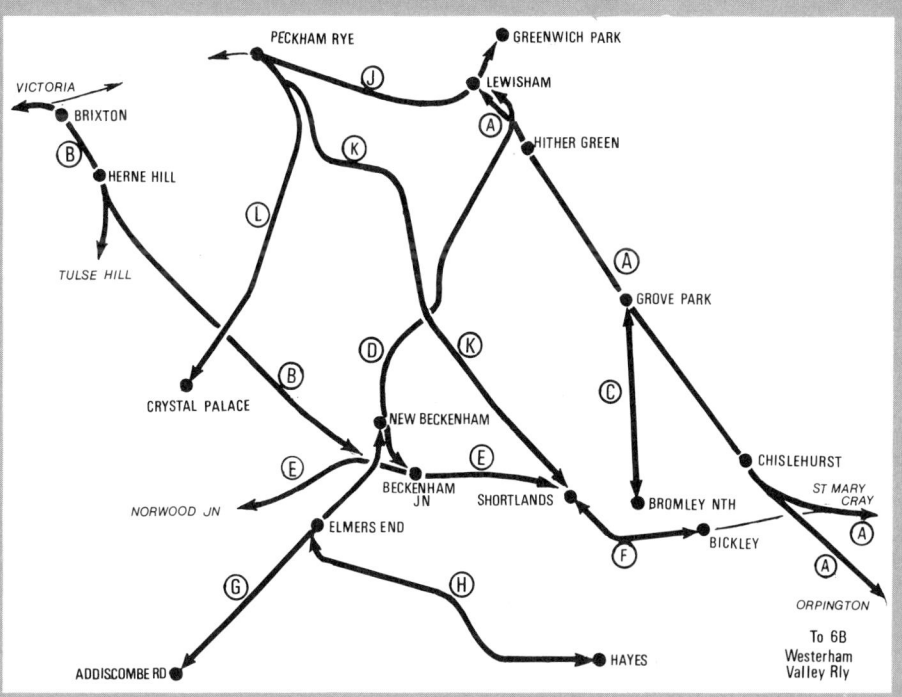

A

SER, Tonbridge line (Western Section)

The Company
South Eastern Railway[a]

Opening dates
St John's–Chislehurst & Bickley Park 01/07/1865
Chislehurst–Seven Oaks (goods) 03/02/1868
Chislehurst–Seven Oaks (ceremonial) 02/03/1868
Chislehurst–Seven Oaks (public) 03/03/1868
Seven Oaks–Tonbridge (jn) (goods) 03/02/1868
Seven Oaks–Tonbridge (local passengers) 01/05/1868
Seven Oaks–Tonbridge (express passengers)
01/06/1868
(Bickley–St Mary Cray 03/12/1860)
Chislehurst Loops:
No 1 (Down Chatham Loop) Chislehurst Jn–LCDR
Jn 19/06/04
No 2 (Up Chatham Loop) St. Mary Cray Jn–Chislehurst
Jn 19/06/04

No 3 (Down Tonbridge Loop) Orpington Jn–LCDR
Jn 08/09/02
No 4 (Up Tonbridge Loop) Orpington Jn–Bickley
Jn 14/09/02
No 4 (Second connection with line west of Bickley
Jn) 14/09/02

Closure Date
No 4 Loop second connection P/G/CC 31/05/14

Lines Remaining Open
St John's–Tonbridge (jn) Pass/Goods
Chislehurst loops Pass/Goods

Remarks
a: See introduction and line 3A for details of Eastern
Section

320	Hither Green*	01/06/1895	Hither Green	†		P/G
321	Grove Park*	01/11/1871	Grove Park	04/12/61†		P
322	Elmstead*®	01/07/04	Elmstead Woods	—		P
323	Chislehurst & Bickley Park*®	01/07/1865	02/03/1868	—		02/03/1868
324	Chislehurst*	02/03/1868	Chislehurst	CDO 26/04/65		P
				18/11/68†		
325	Petts Wood	09/07/28	Petts Wood	CDO 02/11/64		P
				07/10/68		
326	Orpington*	02/03/1868	Orpington	07/10/68†		P
327	Chelsfield	02/03/1868	Chelsfield	18/04/64		P
328	Halstead for Knockholt*®	01/05/1876	Knockholt	16/05/64		P
329	Dunton Green & Riverhead*®	02/03/1868	Dunton Green	02/04/62		P
330	Seven Oaks*®	02/03/1868	Sevenoaks	CDO 04/09/65		P
				02/10/72		
331	Hildenborough	01/05/1868	Hildenborough	05/12/60		P

Notes to table

320 Continental freight depot O 10/10/60, closed 27/12/80. Marshalling yard remains as recessing sidings; HG diesel depot on freight loop to Lee Jn; permanent way sidings and private sidings

321 Grove Park EMU depot

322 ℝ Elmstead Woods 01/10/08

323 ℝ Chislehurst 01/09/1866. Station resited when line extended to Sevenoaks in 1868

324 Amey Roadstone Corporation aggregate terminal

326 ON Orpington EMU depot

328 ℝ Knockholt 01/10/00

329 ℝ Dunton Green 01/07/1873. G 02/04/62 except private sidings since closed

330 ℝ Sevenoaks —/04/1869t; ℝ Sevenoaks (Tubs Hill) 01/08/1869. Various sources give other variations: ℝ Sevenoaks & Riverhead 01/07/1873; ℝ Sevenoaks (Tubs Hill) & Riverhead —/06/1875; ℝ Sevenoaks (Tubs Hill) 1880; ℝ Sevenoaks (Tubs Hill) —/07/1890; ℝ Sevenoaks (Tubs Hill) —/07/01; Final renaming took place in 1950: ℝ Sevenoaks 05/06/50. Carriage sidings at station

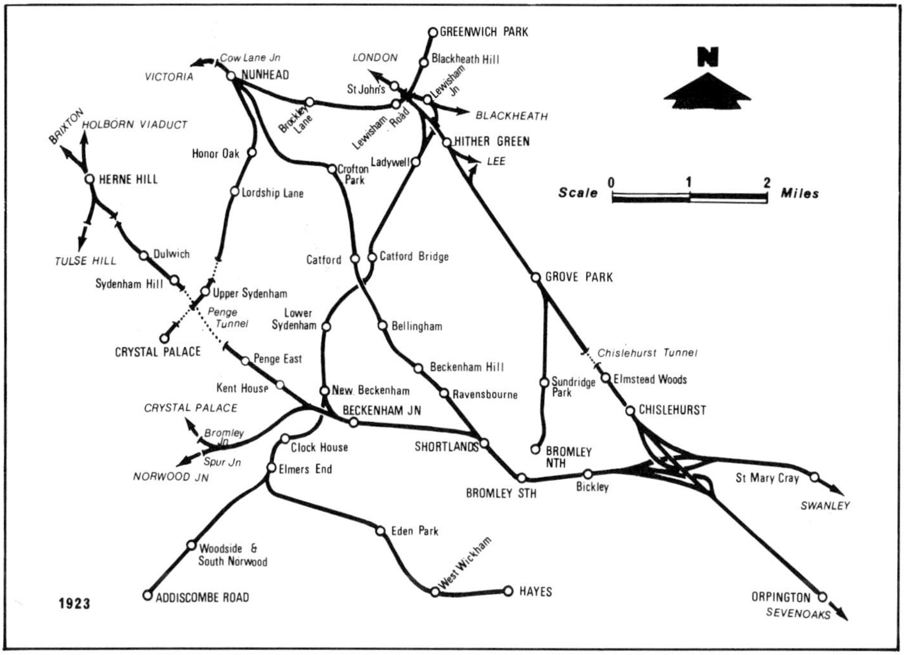

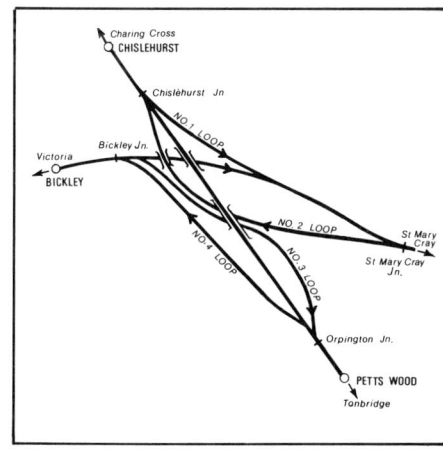

Left:
6A321 Grove Park was opened in 1871, six years after the main SER line, but by the time this photograph was taken in 1888 the spacious station had become a junction with the construction of the Bromley North branch.

Top:
6A321 A few years on, and Grove Park was sporting a somewhat different appearance under SE&CR control.

Above:
6A327 Wartime damage causes some permanent way problems at Chelsfield in 1940. The station opened in 1868 with the main line.

Above:
6A328 Knockholt station (originally Halstead for Knockholt) was opened in 1876 at the summit of the 12-mile climb from New Cross.

Below:
6A330 Class 202 6L Hastings six-car unit No 1019 stands at Sevenoaks with an up train to Charing Cross in June 1979. *Quentin Williamson*

Below:
6A330 The SER's main line station at Sevenoaks (Tubs Hill) with steam and electric traction standing side by side. The engine is Class C 0-6-0 No 31510.

Bottom:
6A330 Sevenoaks down sidings in August 1984, with electro-diesel No 73.110 shunting withdrawn 4-EPB units. *Keith Dungate*

Below:
6A330   Heavy freight locomotive No 56.065 attempts to restart after an engine shut-down at Sevenoaks while working a Mountsorrel to Bat and Ball stone train in April, 1985.   *Keith Dungate*

B

Westerham Valley Railway

The Company
Incorporated 1876
Vested in SER 1881

Opening Dates
Dunton Green (jn)–Westerham (official) 06/07/1881,
(public) 07/07/1881

Closure Date
Dunton Green (jn)–Westerham P/G/CC 30/10/61

Lines Remaining Open
None

332	Chevening Halt	16/04/06	30/10/61	—	30/10/61
333	Brasted*®	07/07/1881	30/10/61	30/10/61	30/10/61
334	Westerham*	07/07/1881	30/10/61	30/10/61	30/10/61

Notes to table
333 ® Brasted Halt and unstaffed from 19/09/55.
Brasted siding G/CC 30/10/61
334 Locomotive shed closed 1906

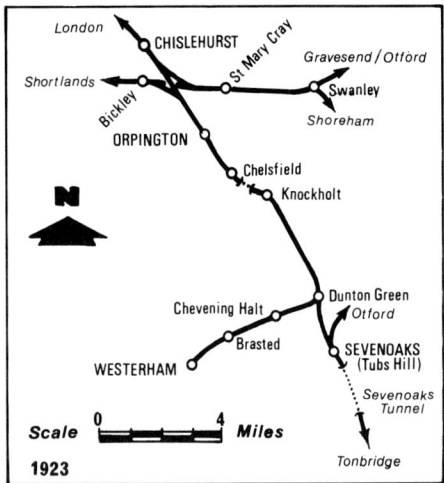

London
CHISLEHURST
St Mary Cray
Gravesend / Otford
Shortlands
Swanley
Bickley
Shoreham
ORPINGTON
Chelsfield
Knockholt

N

Dunton Green
Chevening Halt
Otford
Brasted
SEVENOAKS
WESTERHAM
(Tubs Hill)
Sevenoaks
Tunnel

Scale 0 ——— 4 Miles

1923

Tonbridge

Below:
6B333 The unimposing station at Brasted on the Westerham Valley line opened in 1881 and was unstaffed from 1955. It closed with the branch line in 1961.

Right:
6B334 Westerham was the epitomy of a rural branch terminus, opened in 1881 by the SER. Class H 0-4-4T No 31308 with its two-coach train was typical of passenger services on the branch until its demise in 1961.

Above:
6B334   A buffer-stop view of Westerham, showing the track layout of the attractive country terminus.

C

Bromley Direct Railway

The Company
Incorporated 1874
Vested in SER 1879

Opening Date
Grove Park (jn)–Bromley 01/01/1878

Closure Date
Grove Park (jn)–Bromley G 20/05/68

Line remaining open
Grove Park (jn)–Bromley North Pass

335	Plaistow*®	01/01/1878	Sundridge Park	—	P
336	Bromley*®	01/01/1878	Bromley North	CDO 10/08/64	P
				20/05/68	

Notes to table
335 Plaistow was originally a private halt opened for Sir Edward Scott, a local resident. The station was rebuilt and opened to the public on 01/07/1894 as Sundridge Park

336 ® Bromley North 01/07/1899

Above:
6C335 The exterior of Sundridge Park station, opened as a private halt called Plaistow in 1878 and rebuilt in 1894.

Top right:
6C336 The SER opened their branch line to Bromley in 1878 and the station was renamed Bromley North in 1899.

Bottom right:
6C336 An interesting view of the turntable at Bromley North taken when the station was under SE&CR control.

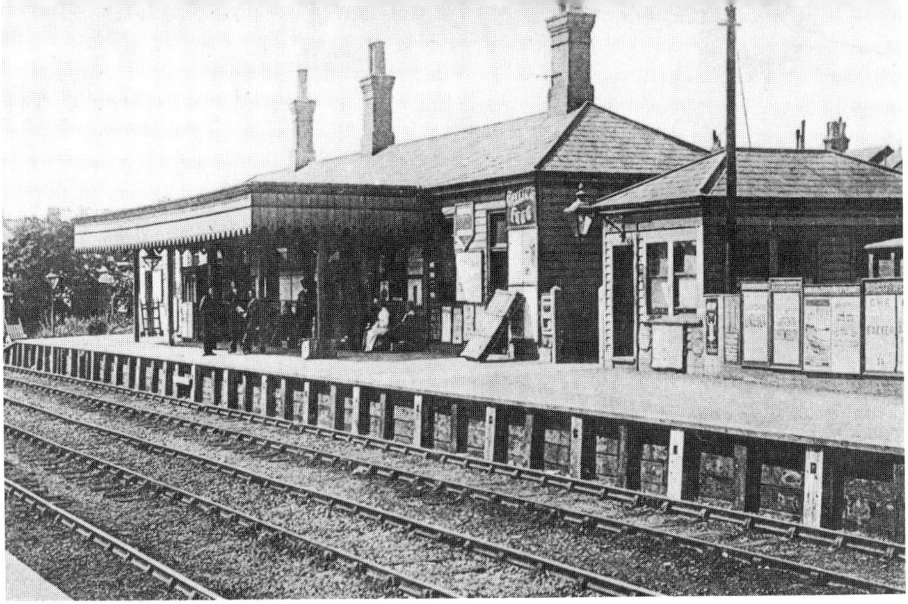

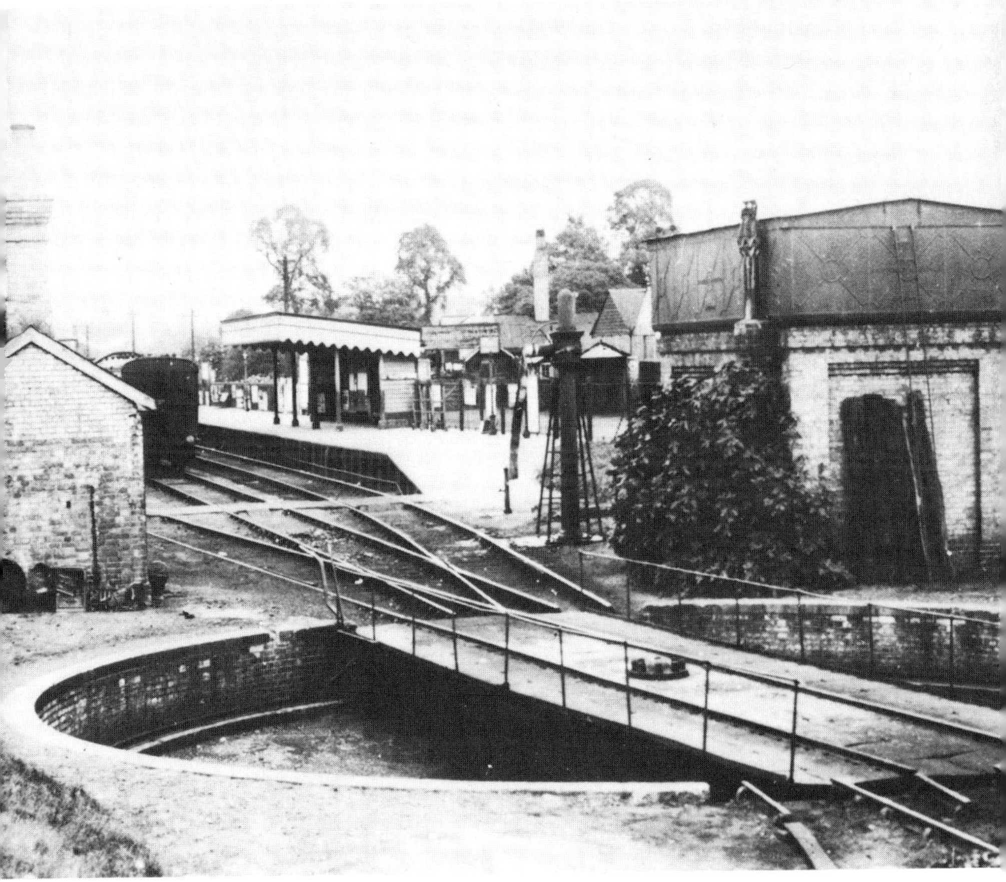

D

Mid-Kent Railway

The Company
Incorporated 1855
Absorbed into SER 1864

Opening Dates
Lewisham Junction–Beckenham (Junction) 01/01/1857
Parks Bridge Jn (St John's)–Ladywell (jn) ––/09/1866
Nunhead loop (Lewisham Rd–Lewisham Jn) (goods)
  07/07/29[a]
Nunhead loop (Lewisham Rd–Lewisham Jn) (pass)
  30/09/35[a]
Courthill Loop Jn North (Lewisham Jn)–Courthill Loop
Jn South (Hither Green) G 07/07/29, P 07/07/30 (steam)
  P/G 16/07/33 (electric)

Closure Date
New Beckenham–Beckenham Junction (Loop) P date
  unknown

Lines Remaining open
Lewisham–New Beckenham Pass/Goods
Beckenham Junction Pass/Goods
New Beckenham–Beckenham Junction (loop) Goods

Remarks
a: This loop to the City took over part of the old closed
  Nunhead line

337	Ladywell	01/01/1857	Ladywell	—		P
338	Catford Bridge	01/01/1857	Catford Bridge	CDO 28/12/64 23/03/68		P
339	Lower Sydenham [1st]*	01/01/1857	1906	unaffected		see entry below
340	Lower Sydenham [2nd]*	1906	Lower Sydenham	20/06/66		P
341	New Beckenham [1st]*	01/04/1864	1864-7	—		1864-7
342	New Beckenham [2nd]*	1864-7	New Beckenham	—		P
343b	Beckenham*®	01/01/1857	Beckenham Junction	†		P/G

Notes to table
339 Replaced by new station
340 See 339. G 20/06/66 except private sidings since closed

341 Replaced by new station to the north
342 See 341
343b ® Beckenham Junction 01/04/1864. See 6E for details of Norwood–Bromley line

E

West End of London & Crystal Palace Railway (Farnborough Extension)

The Company
WEL&CPR 1853[a]
Farnborough extension leased to LCDR 1859
Absorbed into LCDR 1862

Opening Dates
Norwood (Bromley Junction)–Bromley (Shortlands)
  03/05/1858
(LBSCR loop to Spur Junction 18/06/1862)

Closure Dates
(LBSCR loop to Spur Junction P/G/CC Regular traffic
11/09/59, taken out of use 30/10/66[b])

Lines Remaining Open
Bromley Jn (Norwood)–Shortlands Pass/Goods

Remarks

a: Farnborough extension worked and managed by LBSCR

b: Bromley Jn–Penge Jn closed 1915. Re-opened and electrified 1929

343a	Birkbeck	02/03/30	Birkbeck	—		P
343b	Beckenham*	see 6D	see 6D	see 6D		see 6D
344	Bromley*®	03/05/1858	Shortlands	—		P

Notes to table

343b For full details see line 6D

344 ® Shortlands 01/07/1858

F

Mid-Kent (Bromley & St Mary Cray) Railway

The Company
Incorporated 1856
Leased to LCDR 1862

Opening Date
Shortlands–Southborough Road (Bickley) 05/07/1858

Closure Dates
None

Line Remaining Open
Shortlands–Bickley Pass/Goods

345	Bromley*®	22/11/1858	Bromley South	18/04/64	P
346	Southborough Road*®	05/07/1858	Bickley	16/05/64	P

345 ® Bromley South 01/07/1899

346 ® Bickley 01/10/1860. G 16/05/64 except private sidings since closed

6F345 Bo-Bo diesel No 33.025 *Sultan* heads through Bromley South with the 05.22 ballast train from Tonbridge to Bickley in July 1984. The station opened as plain Bromley in 1858. *Keith Dungate*

G

SER, Addiscombe Road branch

The Company
South Eastern Railway[a]

Opening date
New Beckenham–Croydon (Addiscombe Rd)
01/04/1864

Closure Date
Woodside–Addiscombe G 17/06/68

Line Remaining Open
New Beckenham–Addiscombe Pass/Goods[b]

Remarks
a: See introduction
b: Except Woodside–Addiscombe section, closed to goods

347	Clock House	—/06/1890	Clock House	19/04/65	P
348	Elmers End	01/04/1864	Elmers End	06/05/63	P
349	Woodside*®	—/—/1871	Woodside	30/09/63	P
350	Croydon (Addiscombe Road)*®	01/04/1864	Addiscombe	17/06/68†	P

Notes to table
349 ® Woodside & South Norwood 01/10/08;
® Woodside 02/10/44

350 ® Croydon (Addiscombe) 01/04/25;
® Addiscombe (Croydon) 28/02/26;
® Addiscombe 13/06/55. Addiscombe EMU depot

H

West Wickham & Hayes Railway

The Company
Incorporated 1880
Absorbed into SER 1881

Opening Date
Elmers End–Hayes G 29/05/1882

Closure Date
Elmers End–Hayes G 19/04/65

Line Remaining Open
Elmers End–Hayes Pass

6H353 The Hayes branch opened in 1882 and maintained its rural atmosphere in SE&CR days. The station buildings were rebuilt by the Southern Railway, and again after wartime bombing, and today the commuter terminus has lost its goods yard (1965), signalbox and turntable.

351	Eden Park	29/05/1882	Eden Park	—	P
352	West Wickham	29/05/1882	West Wickham	CDO 01/12/61 02/09/63	P
353	Hayes*®	29/05/1882	Hayes	CDO 01/12/61 19/04/65	P

Notes to table
353 ® Hayes (Kent) but later reverted to Hayes – it is thought the word 'Kent' never actually appeared on station signs. Station buildings reconstructed after bomb damage during World War 2

J

LCDR, Greenwich branch

The Company
London, Chatham & Dover Railway[a]

Opening Dates
Nunhead–Blackheath Hill 18/09/1871
Blackheath Hill–Greenwich 01/10/1888
Lewisham–Nunhead loop Goods 07/07/29[b],
Pass 30/09/35[b]

Closure Dates
Nunhead–Greenwich Park P 01/01/17
Brockley Lane–Greenwich Park G/CC 01/01/17

Nunhead–Brockley Lane G 04/05/70[c]

Line Remaining Open
Lewisham–Nunhead loop Pass/Goods[b]

Remarks
a: See introduction
b: The section of line between Lewisham and Nunhead was re-opened with the laying of the loop line, which gave a new alternative route to the city
c: Goods services remained to the GNR coal depot at Brockley Lane until 04/05/70

6J357 The LC&DR started their branch line to Greenwich in 1871, but the last section was not completed until 1888. Martley's Class D 0-4-4WT No 99, *Mona*, rests at Greenwich not long after the station opened. It became Greenwich Park in 1900 and the branch closed in 1917.

354	Brockley Lane*	—/06/1872	01/01/17	04/05/70	04/05/70
355	Lewisham Road	18/09/1871	01/01/17	—	01/01/17
356	Blackheath Hill	18/09/1871	01/01/17	—	01/01/17
357	Greenwich*®	01/10/1888	01/01/17	—	01/01/17

Notes to table
354 CDO at date of closure. LNWR coal depot leased
pte sdgs O 1885. GNR Coal Depot O 1882
357 ® Greenwich Park 01/07/00

K

Shortlands & Nunhead Railway

The Company
Incorporated 1889
Vested in LCDR 01/06/1896[a]

Opening Date
Nunhead–Bromley (jn) 01/07/1892

Closure Dates
None

Line Remaining Open
Nunhead–Shortlands Pass/Goods

Remarks
a: Now known as the Catford loop

358	Crofton Park	01/07/1892	Crofton Park	—	P
359	Catford	01/07/1892	Catford	—	P
360	Bellingham*®	01/07/1892	Bellingham	CDO 28/12/64	P
				25/03/68	
361	Beckenham Hill*	01/07/1892	Beckenham Hill	—	P
362	Ravensbourne	01/07/1892	Ravensbourne	04/09/61	P

Notes to table
360 ® Bellingham (Kent) but later reverted to
Bellingham – it is thought the word "Kent" never
actually appeared on station signs

361 Carriage sidings laid down when Crystal Palace
High Level branch was closed, but since closed

L

Crystal Palace & South London Junction Railway (Southern Section)

The Company
Incorporated 1862
Southern section transferred to LCDR 1875

Closure Dates
Nunhead–Crystal Palace (High Level) P/G/CC 20/09/54[a]

Line Remaining Open
(Brixton)–Peckham Rye–Nunhead Pass/Goods

Opening Dates
Cow Lane Jn (LBSCR)–Crystal Palace 01/08/1865
(Canterbury Rd Jn (Brixton)–Cow Lane Jn (LBSCR)
01/08/1865)

Remarks
a: Line TC 01/01/17, RO 01/03/19; TC 22/05/44, RO
04/03/46

363	Nunhead [1st]*	01/09/1871	03/05/25	unaffected	see entry below
364	Nunhead [2nd]*	03/05/25	Nunhead	02/04/62	P
365	Honor Oak*	—/12/1865	20/09/54	20/09/54	20/09/54
366	Lordship Lane*	01/09/1865	20/09/54	—	20/09/54
367	Upper Sydenham*	01/08/1884	20/09/54	—	20/09/54
368	Crystal Palace (High Level)*®	01/08/1865	20/09/54	20/09/54	20/09/54

Notes to table
363 Replaced by new station slightly to north TC
01/01/17, RO 01/03/19
364 See 363
365 TC 01/01/17, RO 01/03/19, TC 22/05/44,
RO 04/03/46

366 See 365
367 See 365
368 See 365. ® Crystal Palace (High Level) & Upper
Norwood 01/11/1898

6L367 The last years of the Crystal Palace High Level
branch: Southern Region 4-SUB EMU No 4671 enters
Upper Sydenham station in its original livery. The
station opened 20 years after the line in 1884 and
closed in 1954.

Above:
6L368 A forlorn view from the wooden platform of Crystal Palace (High Level) taken after closure in 1954.

Below:
6L368 An external view of the imposing and unusual entrance to the LC&DR's High Level station at Crystal Palace, opened in 1865.

7

Victoria and South London

Contents

Appendices

I   Early Railways
II   The LBSCR
III   The West London Extension Railway
IV   The East London Joint Railway

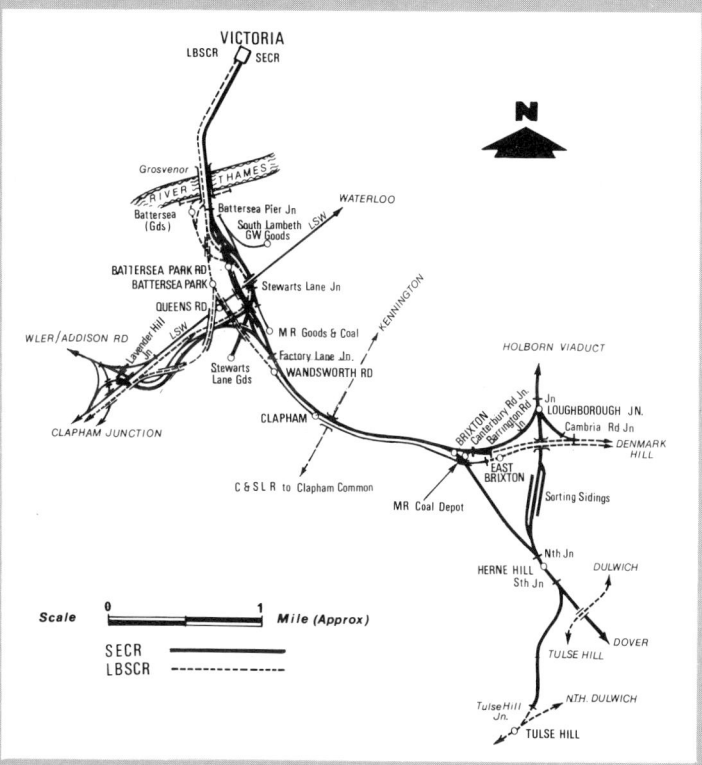

A

Approaches to Victoria

The Company
Victoria Station & Pimlico Railway, Incorporated 1858[a]
Merged into Southern Railway 1921

Opening Dates
Stewarts Lane Junction–Victoria (VS&P line, later
  LBSCR) 01/10/1860[a]
LCDR section of station 25/08/1862[a]
Stewarts Lane Jn–Victoria (LCDR low level line)
  20/12/1866[b]
Factory Jn–Battersea Pier Jn (LCDR high level line)
  01/05/1867[b]
(Stewarts Lane Jn–Herne Hill (LCDR) 25/08/1862)
Factory Jn–Longhedge Jn–Lavender Hill Jn (LCDR line)
  03/04/1866[c,f]
Stewarts Lane Jn–Longhedge Jn (LCDR line) not
  known[c]
(Battersea Pier Jn–Loughborough Park (East Brixton)
  LBSCR South London Line 01/05/1867)[d]
(Pouparts Jn–York Rd Jn (LBSCR high level line)
  01/12/1867)
Stewarts Lane–Longhedge Works (LCDR) 07/10/1865[c]
(Wandsworth Common–Battersea Wharf (West End of
  London & Crystal Palace Railway; later LBSCR)
  29/03/1858)[e]
(Battersea Wharf extension. LBSCR 30/04/1862)[e]

Closure Dates
Stewarts Lane Jn–Victoria, LCDR low level line P date
  unknown

7A370 Empty pullman stock is removed to Stewarts
Lane from platform 7 at Victoria by freight-only diesel
No 47341 in September 1984. The previous day the
pullman train had visited Hollingbourne on an evening
charter. *Keith Dungate*

Stewarts Lane Jn–Pimlico P 01/10/1860
Stewarts Lane Junction–Battersea Wharf G 04/05/70

Lines Remaining Open
Victoria–Factory Jn (via High Level line)–Herne Hill
  Pass/Goods
Battersea Pier Jn–Pouparts Jn Pass/Goods
Battersea Pier Jn–Denmark Hill (South London line)
  Pass/Goods
Battersea Pier Jn–Stewarts Ln Jn–Longhedge
  Jn–Lavender Hill/Latchmere Jns Goods

Remarks
a: The line between Victoria and Stewarts Lane
   Junction was built by the Victoria Station & Pimlico
   Railway but used by the LBSCR and LCDR from its
   inception. Financial agreements allotted the LBSCR
   half of Victoria station, the other half being jointly
   leased to the LCDR and GWR. The GWR did not
   obtain access, however, until the West London
   Extension Railway was opened on 02/03/1863 LCD
   trains used temporary station from 03/12/1860 until
   permanent station at Victoria was brought into use
   on 25/08/1862
b: The LCDR station at Stewarts Lane closed on
   01/01/1867 and the LCDR low level route to Victoria
   subsequently became goods only. Alternative
   sources give O date as 01/01/1867 for LCDR HL line
c: Opened only for goods
d: Under an 1863 Act, it was arranged that the LBSCR
   would construct four tracks between Barrington
   Road Junction and Cow Lane Jn (Peckham), while
   the LCDR would construct a new line between
   Barrington Rd Jn and Factory Junction. In both
   cases, the southern pair of tracks would be used by
   the LBSCR and the northern by the LCDR. Both
   junctions were points of demarcation. Thus the

nominally LBSCR stations at Denmark Hill and Peckham Rye were built to allow LCDR use of the northern platforms. Timetables show the LCDR platforms as being opened on 01/08/1865, with the line, but work on the stations was not completed until the LBSCR South London line came into use on 13/08/1866 between London Bridge and Loughborough Park. The LBSCR stations at York Road, Wandsworth Road, Clapham and Loughborough Park all opened on 01/05/1867 with the western section of the South London Line. York Road was ® York Road & Battersea Park 01/11/1870, ® Battersea Park & York Rd 01/01/1877 and finally ® Battersea Park on 01/06/1885. Battersea Park, Wandsworth Rd, Clapham, Denmark Hill and Peckham Rye all remain open to passengers.

Loughborough Park was ® Loughborough Park & Brixton —/01/1870t®; 05/01/76 East Brixton on 01/01/1894 and closed completely on 05/01/76

e: The West End of London and Crystal Palace Railway opened to Battersea Wharf on 29/03/1858 with passenger stations at Stewarts Lane (LBSCR) and Pimlico. Pimlico closed on 01/10/1860 and Stewarts Lane on 01/12/1858; neither had freight facilities. Battersea Wharf, the goods depot, closed to freight on 04/05/70. The WEL&CP Railway was incorporated in 1853 and the Battersea Wharf line leased to the LBSCR in 1858 and bought by the company in 1859.

f: An alternative source gives 01/07/1865 as the opening date for the LCDR link between Longhedge Jn and Factory Jn

369	Victoria (LBSCR)*	01/10/1860	Victoria	—†	P
370	Victoria (LCDR)*	25/08/1862	Victoria	—†	P
371	Grosvenor Road (LBSCR)*	01/11/1870	01/04/07	—	01/04/07
372	Grosvenor Road (LCDR)	01/01/1867	01/10/11	—	01/10/11
373	Battersea Park (York Road) (LCDR)*®	01/05/1867	03/04/16	—	03/04/16

Notes to table

369 Carriage sidings and Grosvenor EMU depot. LBSCR station opened with VS&PR line from Stewarts Lane Junction. The two separate stations were connected in 1924

370 See 369

371 LBSCR platforms used for ticket collecting from 1867

373 Opened with LCDR high level line. ® Battersea Park Road 01/11/1877. An LBSCR station was opened at Battersea on 01/10/1860, also known as Battersea Pier. It was ® Battersea Park 01/07/1862 and closed completely on 01/11/1870

B

LCDR, Herne Hill line

The Company
London, Chatham & Dover Railway[a]

Opening Dates
Stewarts Lane Junction–Herne Hill 25/08/1862[b]
Herne Hill–Beckenham (Penge Jn) 01/07/1863
Herne Hill–Tulse Hill Jn (LBSCR connection) 01/01/1869
(Brixton–Loughborough Jn 01/05/1863)
(Canterbury Rd Jn–Cow Lane Jn (LBSCR) 01/08/1865)
(Herne Hill–Elephant & Castle 06/10/1862)

Closure Dates
Stewarts Lane Jn–Factory Jn P date unknown
Brixton–Loughborough Jn P 03/04/16

Lines Remaining open
Stewarts Lane Jn–Herne Hill–Beckenham (Penge Jn) Goods
Factory Jn–Herne Hill–Beckenham (Penge Jn) Pass
Brixton–Loughborough Jn Goods
Herne Hill–Tulse Hill Jn, Canterbury Rd Jn–Cow Lane Jn Pass/Goods
Herne Hill–Elephant & Castle Pass/Goods

Remarks
a: See introduction
b: See 7A for details of stations

374	Stewarts Lane*	01/05/1863	01/01/1867	02/11/70†	02/11/70
375	Wandsworth Road*	01/03/1863	03/04/16	N/A	N/A
376	Clapham & North Stockwell*®	25/08/1862	03/04/16	10/6/63	10/06/63
377	Brixton & South Stockwell*®	25/08/1862	Brixton	—	P
378	Herne Hill	25/08/1862	Herne Hill	01/08/66	P

379	Dulwich*®	—/10/1863	West Dulwich	—	P
380	Sydenham Hill	—/08/1863	Sydenham Hill	—	P
381	Penge*®	01/07/1863	Penge East	CDO 30/11/64	P
				07/11/66	
382	Kent House*	01/10/1884	Kent House	—	P

Notes to table

374 Temporary station, closed 01/01/1867. Goods depot at Stewarts Lane closed 02/11/70 except for private sidings and electro-diesel depot (SL). The steam shed replaced depots at Battersea (LBSCR) and Longhedge (SEC) and nearby was Longhedge Works (LCDR). South Lambeth (GWR) Goods depot O 01/01/13

375 LBSCR side of station remains open. MR Coal depot O 1874 Wandsworth Road

376 LBSCR side of station remains open. ® Clapham Road & North Stockwell —/05/1895; ® Clapham & North Stockwell —/06/14; ® Clapham 27/09/37

377 ® Brixton. MR Coal depot O 1876 CC 1946

379 ® West Dulwich 20/09/26

381 Listed as Penge Lane in Bradshaw 1864-1869, ® Penge East 09/07/23. For details of line opening, also see line 7A

382 Spur line between Kent House and what is now Birkbeck was built by LCDR under powers obtained in 1874. It was completed by 1879 but never used for regular passenger trains, although specials may have used it occasionally. It was closed as a through running line by 1895, but was used for some years as a siding, with access from the Kent House direction

Appendix I:

Early Railways

Surrey Iron Railway
Incorporated 21/05/1801
Wandsworth–Croydon 0 (goods only) 26/07/1803
Hackbridge branch 0 (goods only) 01/06/1804
Line closed completely 31/08/1846

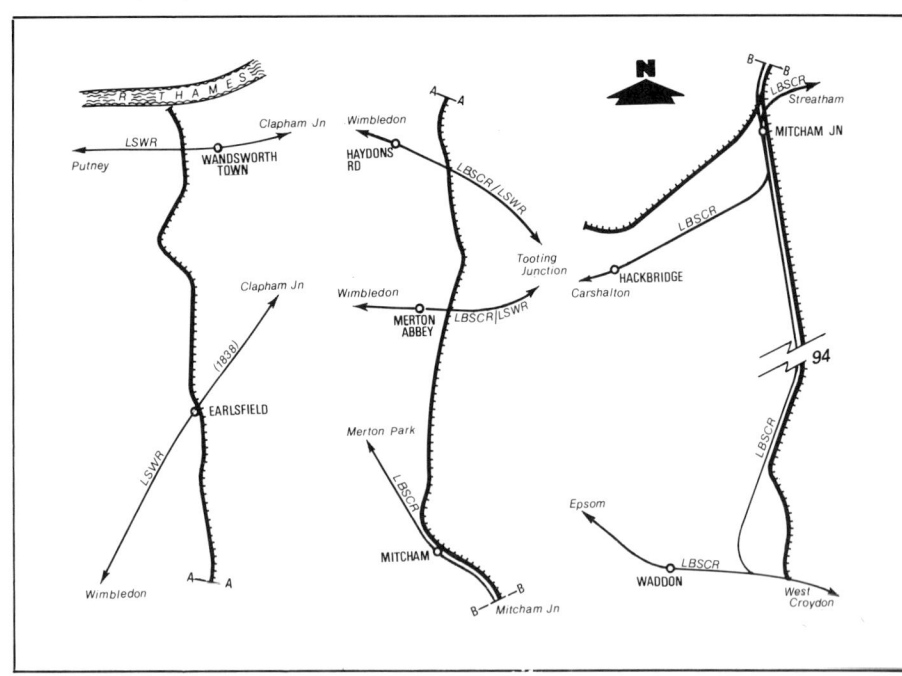

Croydon, Merstham & Godstone Railway
Incorporated 17/05/1803
Croydon – Greystone Lime Works (Merstham) 0 (goods
only) 24/07/1805

Canal basin branch 0 (goods only) 1809
Bought by L&BR 1838
Completely closed 1839-40
Company dissolved (C,M&GR) 01/07/1839

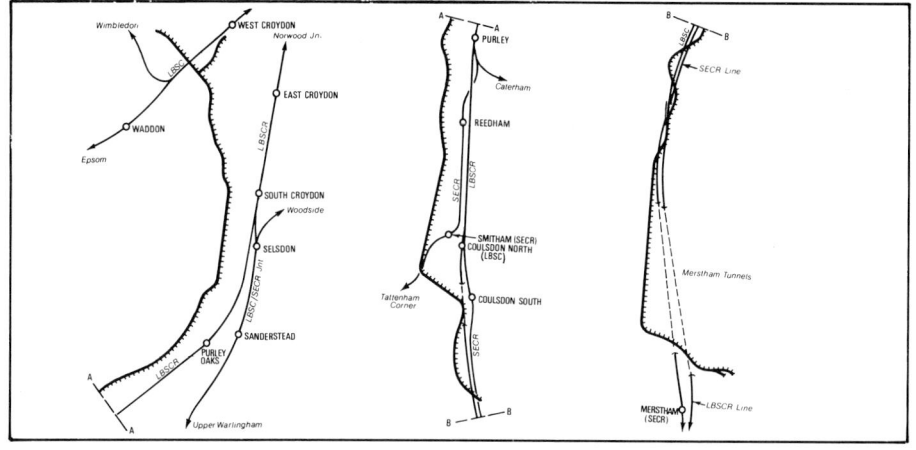

Appendix II:
Companies Amalgamated to Form LBSCR

Royal assent was given on 27/07/1846 for the
amalgamation of five railway companies to form the
London, Brighton & South Coast Railway.
Constituent railways were: London & Croydon

Railway, London & Brighton Railway; Brighton &
Chichester Railway; Croydon & Epsom Railway;
Brighton, Lewes & Hastings Railway.

Appendix III:
The Formation of the WLER

The West London Extension Railway was incorporated
in 1859 as a joint company in which four railways had
part ownership.

The joint shares were as follows: LNWR one-third;
GWR one-third; LSWR one-sixth; LBSCR one-sixth.

Appendix IV:
The Formation of the ELJR

The East London Joint Railway was jointly owned by
five railway companies who had equal shares in the
company. The SER took over maintenance of the ELJR
on 01/07/1885, although the management of the

railway was taken over by the Metropolitan Railway in
01/07/21 and the maintenance on 01/01/24.
    The companies who had shares in the railway were:
SE&CR; LBSCR; GER; MetRy; Met-District Rly.

Further Reading

Maps

Baker, S.	Rail Atlas of Britain and Ireland, 4th Ed	OPC, 1984
Wignall, C. J.	British Railways Maps & Gazetteer 1830-1981	OPC, 1983
—	Pre-Grouping Atlas and Gazetteer,	Ian Allan, 1976

Closures

Clark, R. H.	Southern Region Record,	Oakwood Press, 1964
Clinker, C. R.	Clinker's Register of Closed Passenger Stations and Goods Depots in England, Scotland and Wales, 1830-1977,	Avon Anglia, 1978
Daniels, G. and Dench, L. A.	Passengers No More,	Ian Allan, 1973
Greville, M. D. and Spence, J.	Closed Passenger Lines of Great Britain,	Railway & Canal Historical Soc.
Klapper, C.	London's Lost Railways,	Routledge & Kegan Paul, 1976
Searle, M.	Lost Lines,	New Cavendish Books, 1982

Lines

Bayliss, D.	The Surrey Iron Railway,	Railway Magazine, July 1978
Bennett, A. R.	The First Railway in London,	Conway Maritime Press, 1971
Bone, D. A.	Oxted Line Relived,	Railway Magazine, July 1971
Burnham, T. G.	Branch to Bromley North,	Railway Magazine, Feb 1975
Catt, A. R.	The East Kent Railway,	Oakwood 1975
Course, E. A.	The Bexley Heath Railway,	Woolwich & District Antiquarian Proceedings, Vol XXX, 1954
Course, E. A.	London's Railways,	Batsford, 1962
Davies, W. J. K.	The Romney, Hythe & Dymchurch Railway,	David & Charles, 1975
Devereux, C.	Railways to Sevenoaks,	Oakwood, 1977
Fellows, Rev. R.	History of the Canterbury & Whitstable Railway	J. A. Jennings, 1930
Fenton, M.	Branch to Sheerness,	Railway Magazine, Mar 1982
Garrett, S. R.	The Kent & East Sussex Railway,	Oakwood, 1972
Gould, D.	The Westerham Valley Branch,	Oakwood, 1974
Gray, A.	Branch to Chatham Central,	Railway Magazine, Sep 1976
Gray, A.	The London to Brighton Line 1841-1977	Oakwood, 1977
Gray, A.	Isle of Grain Railways,	Oakwood, 1974
Hilton, J.	A History of the South Eastern & Chatham Railway, Vols 1-3.	John Hilton,
Jackman, M.	The Bricklayers Arms Branch & Loco Shed,	Oakwood,1980
Jackson, A.	Rails to Tattenham Corner,	Railway Magazine, Jun 1975
Kidner, R. W.	The Dartford Loop Line 1866-1966,	Oakwood, 1966
Kidner, R. W.	The Reading to Tonbridge Line,	Oakwood, 1974
Kidner, R. W.	The South Eastern & Chatham Railway,	Oakwood, 1963
Kidner, R. W.	The Oxted Line,	Oakwood, 1972
Lee, C. E.	Useful but Unloved: Ludgate Hill Station,	Railway Magazine, Dec 1964
Lee, C. E.	Charing Cross Station, 1864-1964,	Railway Magazine, Jan 1964
Lee, C. E.	Cannon Street Station, 1866-1966,	Railway Magazine, Aug 1966
Lee, C. E.	Victoria Station in the 19th Century,	Railway Magazine, Sep 1960
MacDonald, J. D.	The Dover & Martin Mill Railway,	Railway Magazine No 572
Maxted, I.	The Canterbury & Whitstable Railway,	Oakwood, 1970
Orford, V. W.	The Connections at Lewisham, SR,	Railway Magazine, Feb 1930
Owen, N.	The Tattenham Corner Branch,	Oakwood, 1978
Ross, P.	A Romney Album	RHDR
Rugman, W. J.	The Croydon & Oxted Joint and Woodside & South Croydon Railways,	Railway World No 416
Searle, M. V.	Down the line to Dover	Midas Books, 1983
Scott-Morgan, J.	The Colonel Stephens Railways,	David & Charles, 1978
Snell, J. B.	One Man's Railway (The RH&DR),	David & Charles, 1983
Spindler, F. G.	The Canterbury & Whitstable Railway,	Railway Magazine No LXVI
Thomas, R. H. G.	London's First Railway, The London & Greenwich Railway,	Batsford, 1972
Treby, E.	The Croydon Canal and its Railway Successors,	Railway Magazine, Oct 1967
Vallance, H. A.	The Bickley & Chislehurst Loops, Southern Railway,	Railway Magazine, Jul 1947

Vallance, H. A.	British Branch Lines,	Batsford, 1965
Wolfe, C. S.	Historical Guide to the Romney, Hythe & Dymchurch Railway,	RHDR Assoc, 1976
Woodman, T.	The Railways to Hayes,	Hayes Village Assoc, 1982
Young, J. N.	Angerstein Wharf,	Railway Magazine, Oct 1973

Engines

Bradley, D. L.	Locomotives of the South Eastern & Chatham Railway,	RCTS, 1961
Bradley, D. L.	The Locomotive History of the London, Chatham & Dover Railway,	RCTS, 1979
Wakeman, N.	The South Eastern & Chatham Railway Locomotive List 1842-1952,	Oakwood, 1953

General

Allen, C. J.	Salute to the Southern,	Ian Allan, 1974
Bilbrough, G. F.	Railway Mileage Tables (Great Britain),	Birmingham Chamber of Commerce, 1924
Body, G.	Railways of the Southern Region,	Patrick Stephens, 1984
Course, E.	The Railways of Southern England: The Main Lines,	Batsford, 1973
Course, E.	The Railways of Southern England: Secondary and Branch lines,	Batsford, 1974
Ganmell, C. J.	The Branch Line Age,	Moorland, 1976
Gould, D.	The South Eastern & Chatham Railway in the 1914-18 War,	Oakwood, 1981
Hasenson, A.	The 'Golden Arrow',	Howard Baker, 1970
Heap, C. and Van Riemsdijk, J	The Pre-Grouping Railways Part 2	HMSO 1980
Klapper, C. F.	Sir Herbert Walker's Southern Railway,	Ian Allan, 1973
Kidner, R. W.	The Southern Railway,	Oakwood, 1958
Nock, O. S.	The South Eastern & Chatham Railway,	Ian Allan
Thomas, D. St. J.	The Country Railway,	Penguin, 1979
Turner J. T.	The London, Brighton & South Coast Railway, vols 1-3,	Batsford, 1977-9
White, H. P.	A Regional History of the Railways of Great Britain: Vol 2: Southern England,	David & Charles, 1969
	Vol 3: Greater London,	David & Charles, 1971

1G37 Sandling Junction with locomotive Nos D6527 and D5002 heading the 12.35 Margate-Charing Cross. The branch to Hythe is on the right. Note the two Pullman cars acting as holiday coaches. *M. Edwards*

Index of Lines

Ownership of Lines by Major Companies

Index of Stations

Station	Line No/Station No	Station	Line No/Station No
Dover (Admiralty Pier)	1J 62	Greatstone-on-sea (Halt)	3E 194
Dover (Bulwark Street)	1J 61a	Greenhithe	5E 301
Dover (Town)	1G 45	Greenwich (temporary station)	5C 280
Dover Harbour (1st station)	1J 60	Greenwich (2nd station)	5C 281
Dover Marine	1J 63	Greenwich (3rd station)	5C 282
Dover Town (Priory)	1J 59	Greenwich (Maze Hill)	5D 283
Dover Town & Harbour (Dover Harbour,		Greenwich (Park)	6J 357
2nd station)	1J 61	Grosvenor Road (LBSCR)	7A 371
Dover Western Docks	1J 63	Grosvenor Road (LCDR)	7A 372
Dulwich (West Dulwich)	7B 379	Grove Ferry	1B 13
Dumpton Park	1D 29	Grove Park	6A 321
Dungeness	3E 192		
Dunton Green (& Riverhead)	6A 329	Halling	2L 153
		Halstead (for Knockholt)	6A 328
Earley	4B 207	Ham Street (& Orlestone)	3B 163
East Farleigh	2K 146	Harrietsham	2J 137
East Malling (Halt)	2H 132	Harty Road Halt	2G 122
East Margate	1C 26	Hastings	3B 171
East Minster-on-sea	2G 119	Hawkhurst	3D 189
Eastchurch	2G 121	Hayes (Kent)	6H 353
Eastry (EKR)	1 Appendix 1	Headcorn	3A 160
Eastry South (EKR)	1 Appendix 1	Headcorn Junction	3 Appendix 2
Ebbsfleet & Cliffsend Halt	1B 14a	Herne Bay (& Hampton-on-sea)	1C 22
Eden Park	6H 351	Herne Hill	7B 378
Edenbridge	4A 201	High Brooms	3C 174
Elephant & Castle	5A 255	High Halden Road	3 Appendix 2
Elham	1K 68	High Halstow Halt	2B 82
Elmers End	6G 348	Higham	2A 76
Elmstead (Woods)	6A 322	Hildenborough	6A 331
Eltham	5F 306b	Hither Green	6A 320
Eltham (& Mottingham)	5H 314	Holborn Viaduct (High Level)	5A 263
Eltham Park	5F 307	Holborn Viaduct (Low Level; Snow Hill)	5A 261
Eltham Well Hall	5F 306a	Hollingbourne	2J 136
Elvington (EKR)	1 Appendix 1	Honor Oak	6L 365
Erith	5E 297	Hoo Staff Halt	2A 75
Etchingham	3C 180	Hope Mill (Goudhurst)	3D 187
Ewell (Kearsney)	1J 58	Horsmonden	3D 186
Eynsford	2H 124	Hothfield (Halt)	2J 140
Eythorne (EKR)	1 Appendix 1	Hurst Green (Halt)	4G 351
		Hythe (Kent)	1H 48
Falconwood	5F 308		
Farnborough (North)	4B 214	Junction Road Halt	3 Appendix 2
Farningham (Road & Sutton-at-Hone)	2D 94		
Faversham	2D 107	Kearsney (Ewell)	1J 58
Fawkham (Longfield)	2D 95	Kemsing	2H 129
Folkestone (temporary station)	1G 41	Kemsley (Halt)	2F 111
Folkestone (Junction; Folkestone East)	1G 43	Kenley	4E 236
Folkestone Central	1G 42	Kent House	7B 382
Folkestone Harbour (1st station)	1G 46	Kidbrooke	5F 305
Folkestone Harbour (2nd station)	1G 47	Kingswood (& Burgh Heath)	4D 233
Folkestone Warren	1G 44	Knockholt	6A 328
Folkestone West	1G 40	Knowlton Halt (EKR)	1 Appendix 1
Frant	3C 177		
Frittenden Road	3 Appendix 2	Ladywell	6D 337
		Lee	5H 313
Gillingham (New Brompton)	2D 102	Leigh (Halt)	4A 203
Godstone	4A 200	Lenham	2J 138
Gomshall & Shere	4B 219	Lewisham (Junction)	5E 288
Goudhurst	3D 187	Lewisham Road	6J 355
Grain	2B 88	Leysdown	2G 123
Grain Crossing Halt	2B 87	London Bridge (L&G)	5C 268
Graveney	1C 18	London Bridge (L&C)	5C 269
Gravesend (G&R station)	2A 70	London Bridge (Joint station)	5C 270
Gravesend (Central)	2A 71	London Bridge (SER New station)	5C 271
Gravesend (West Street; Gravesend West)	2E 110b	London Bridge (LBSCR New station)	5C 272

Station	Line No/Station No
Longfield (Fawkham)	2D 95
Longfield Halt	2E 109a
Lordship Lane	6L 366
Loughborough Road (Loughborough Junction)	5A 252
Lower Sydenham (1st station)	6D 339
Lower Sydenham (2nd station)	6D 340
Ludgate Hill (temporary station)	5A 259
Ludgate Hill (permanent station)	5A 260
Lydd (Town)	3E 191
Lydd-on-sea (Halt)	3E 193
Lyghe Halt	4A 203
Lyminge	1K 69
Miadstone (East)	2H 134
Maidstone (West)	2K 148
Maidstone Barracks	2L 149
Maidstone Road (Paddock Wood)	3A 157
Malling (West Malling)	2H 131
Marden	3A 158
Marden Park (Woldingham)	4G 249
Margate (West)	1C 25
Margate (Sands)	1B 17
Margate East	1C 26
Martin Mill	1F 34
Maze Hill (& East Greenwich)	5D 283
Meopham	2D 97
Merstham (1st station)	4C 225
Merstham (2nd station)	4C 226
Middle Stoke Halt	2B 85
Milton Range Halt	2A 74
Milton Road Halt	2A 72
Minster (Thanet)	1B 14
Minster (Sheppey)	2G 118
Mottingham	5H 314
Mountfield (Halt)	3C 182
New Beckenham (1st station)	6D 341
New Beckenham (2nd station)	6D 342
New Brompton (Gillingham)	2D 102
New Cross	5E 286
New Eltham	5H 315
New Hythe	2L 151
New Romney & Littlestone (-on-sea)	3E 195
Newington	2D 104
North Camp	4B 215
North Kent Junction	5E 285
Northfleet	5E 303
Northiam	3 Appendix 2
Nunhead (1st station)	6L 363
Nunhead (2nd station)	6L 364
Nutfield	4A 199
Ore	3B 170
Orpington	6A 326
Otford	2H 126
Otney	2H 127
Oxted (& Limpsfield)	4G 250
Paddock Wood	3A 157
Penge (East)	7B 381
Penshurst	4A 202
Petts Wood	6A 325
Plaistow (Sundridge Park)	6B 335
Pluckley	3A 161
Plumstead	5E 293

Station	Line No/Station No
Poison Cross (EKR)	1 Appendix 1
Pope Street (New Eltham)	5H 315
Port Victoria	2B 89
Queenborough	2F 113
Queenborough Pier	2F 116
Radnor Park	1G 42
Rainham (& Newington)	2D 103
Ramsgate (SR)	1D 30
Ramsgate (& St Lawrence-on-sea; Ramsgate Harbour)	1C 28
Ramsgate (Town)	1B 16
Reading (SER 1st station)	4B 205
Reading (South)	4B 206
Redhill (Reigate)	4C 228
Red Hill & Reigate Road (Reigate)	4C 227
Reedham (Halt)	4D 229
Reigate (Redhill)	4C 228
Reigate (SER)	4A 198
Reigate (Town)	4B 223
Richborough (EKR)	1 Appendix 1
Richborough Castle Halt	1E 30a
Riddlesdown	4G 247
Robertsbridge	3C 181
Rochester	2D 100
Rochester (G&R)	2A 77
Rochester Bridge	2D 99
Rochester Common	2M 155
Roman Road (EKR)	1 Appendix 1
Rosherville Halt	2E 110a
Rye	3B 165
Rye Harbour	3B 173
Salehurst Halt	3 Appendix 2
Sanderstead	4G 246
Sandgate	1H 49
Sandhurst (temporary station)	4B 211
Sandhurst (permanent station)	4B 212
Sandling (Junction)	1G 37
Sandwich	1E 31
Sandwich Road (EKR)	1 Appendix 1
Selling	1J 50
Selsdon Road	4F 245
Sevenoaks (Bat & Ball)	2H 128
Sevenoaks (Tubs Hill & Riverhead)	6A 330
Sevenoaks Junction (Swanley Junction)	2D 93
Shakespeare Halt	1G 44a
Shalford	4B 217
Sharnal Street	2B 83
Sheerness (Dockyard)	2F 114
Sheerness East	2G 117
Sheerness-on-sea	2F 115
Shepherds Well	1J 56
Shepherds Well (EKR)	1 Appendix 1
Shooters Hill & Eltham Park	5F 307
Shoreham (Kent)	2H 125
Shorncliffe Camp (1st station)	1G 39
Shorncliffe Camp (2nd station; Folkestone West)	1G 40
Shortlands	6E 344
Sidcup	5H 316
Sidley	3F 196
Sindlesham & Hurst Halt (Winnersh)	4B 208
Sittingbourne (& Milton Regis)	2D 105
Slade Green	5E 298

119

Note: Romney, Hythe & Dymchurch Railway stations are not included in the index.